EARLY GOTHIC SAINT-DENIS

EARLY GOTHIC
SAINT-DENIS

RESTORATIONS AND SURVIVALS

PAMELA Z. BLUM

UNIVERSITY OF CALIFORNIA PRESS

BERKELEY   LOS ANGELES   OXFORD

THE PUBLISHER GRATEFULLY ACKNOWLEDGES THE CONTRIBUTION PROVIDED
BY THE ART BOOK FUND OF THE ASSOCIATES OF THE UNIVERSITY OF
CALIFORNIA PRESS, WHICH IS SUPPORTED BY A MAJOR GIFT FROM THE
AHMANSON FOUNDATION.

University of California Press
Berkeley and Los Angeles, California

University of California Press, Ltd.
Oxford, England

Photo credits:
© ARCH. PHOT. S.P.A.D.E.M., Paris / V.A.G.A., New York, 1991: Figs. 2, 3, 5. Bildarchiv Foto
Marburg: Figs. 6a–b, 28, Plates I, Xa–b, XIa–b. Courtesy of The Metropolitan Museum
of Art, New York: Figs. 14, 30a–b.

Library of Congress Cataloging-in-Publication Data

Blum, Pamela Z.
Early Gothic Saint-Denis : restorations and survivals /
Pamela Z. Blum
p.   cm.
Includes bibliographical references and index.
ISBN 0-520-07371-1
1. Sculpture, Gothic—Conservation and restoration—France—Saint-Denis.
2. Sculpture, French—Conservation and restoration—France—Saint-Denis.
3. Christian art and symbolism—Medieval, 500–1500—Conservation and
restoration—France—Saint-Denis. 4. Abbaye de Saint-Denis (Saint-Denis, France)
I. Title.
NB1910.B58 1992
730'.944'362—dc20   91-23849

Printed in the United States of America

9   8   7   6   5   4   3   2   1

The paper used in this publication meets the minimum requirements of
American National Standard for Information Sciences—Permanence of Paper for
Printed Library Materials, ANSI Z39.48-1984. ♾

CONTENTS

ILLUSTRATIONS

FIGURES

PLATES Following page 123

PREFACE

The archaeological study of restorations to the three western portals at Saint-Denis began in summer 1968 under the aegis of the late Sumner McKnight Crosby. Having spent the better part of his professional career studying the architecture of the twelfth-century church and excavating for the remains of earlier structures, he wanted to resolve the differences of opinion about what, if anything, remained of the twelfth-century sculpture on the western portals.* The drastic and stylistically unsympathetic restoration in the nineteenth century by the sculptor Joseph-Sylvestre Brun overshadowed the twelfth-century aesthetic to the point that some critics dismissed the sculptural ensemble as completely restored. Indeed, nineteenth-century heads—crude parodies of the twelfth-century style—offend the informed viewer today no less than they did the few but articulate critics who denounced the restorations. The rhetoric in their diatribes gave support to later critics who believed that none of the original carving had survived.

*See, for example, Emile Mâle in "La Part de Suger dans la création de l'iconographie du Moyen Age," *Revue de l'art ancien et moderne* 35 (1914): 339: "Si pourtant on veut bien triompher d'une répugnance trop légitime, on s'apercevra qu'un des portails, celui de milieu, conserve ses dispositions primitive. Içi, comme ailleurs, les têtes et les mains ont été refaites, les draperies ont été sans doute retouchées mais les grandes lignes de la scène sont restées intactes." (If one can overcome a very legitimate repugnance [because of the restorations], one can see that one of the portals, that in the center, has preserved its original dispositions. Here, as elsewhere, the heads and hands have been redone, the draperies without doubt reworked, but the overall composition of the scene remains intact). Whitney Stoddard's conclusions, later modified on the basis of the archaeological study published in 1973, were entirely the opposite: "Combining documentary and visual evidence, we are forced to eliminate as twelfth-century work all sculpture of the west façade of Saint-Denis except some of the plinths below the former jamb sculptures, fragments preserved in museums in France and the United States, and some of the tympanum and archivolts of the central portal" (W. S. Stoddard, *The West Portals of Saint-Denis and Chartres. Sculpture in the Ile-de-France from 1140–1190* [Cambridge, Mass., 1952], 3. For his revised opinion, see idem, *The Sculptors of the West Portals of Chartres Cathedral* [New York, 1987], 113. See also Chapter 2, n. 30).

Yet Professor Crosby remained certain that vestiges of the twelfth-century sculpture still existed, at least in the central portal. In 1968 he asked me join his archaeological "équipe" and undertake an examination of the portals. Under his auspices I received the necessary permissions to do the research on site. Each year from 1968 through 1973 he arranged for the erection of scaffolding from which I could examine the carved surfaces under magnification, and M. Sallez, architect-in-chief of Saint-Denis, graciously granted his permission for it.

During those same years Professor Crosby subsidized my travel, research, and writing, and finally arranged for the translation and publication in France of an article presenting a condensed version of the findings with respect to the sculpture of the central portal (Sumner McKnight Crosby and Pamela Z. Blum, "Le Portail central de la façade occidentale de Saint-Denis," trans. D. Thibaudat, *Bulletin monumental* 131/3 [1973]: 209–66). I remain deeply grateful to him not only for the opportunity to do the archaeological research but also for the countless ways in which he facilitated my work. My research confirmed his belief that unspoiled twelfth-century sculpture had survived. The generous amount discovered and the high quality of the extant carving more than justified the project.

This book incorporates much of the information in the French article, and I wish to thank to Alain Erlande-Brandenburg for permission to include the material in an English version. Unfortunately space does not permit a detailed analysis of every figure, but an effort will be made to resolve questions and controversies that have arisen concerning the restoration, and emphasis will be given to the figures that best reveal the ideas and aesthetic preferences of the twelfth-century sculptors. With its several additions—introductory background material, notes that take into account recent literature, and an expanded conclusion—the study is no longer addressed exclusively to the scholarly community. The methods employed in the archaeological investigation of the central portal at Saint-Denis are outlined here in full, in hopes that they can instruct a future generation of archaeologists and historians of art concerned not only with medieval sculpture, but also with that of other periods.

PAMELA Z. BLUM

New Haven, Connecticut

November, 1990

CHAPTER 1

SAINT-DENIS IN HISTORY

Often called the cradle of Gothic art, Saint-Denis provides documentation crucial to an understanding of the formative period of the Gothic style in the Ile-de-France. In the 1130s and 1140s, Abbot Suger (1122–1151) sponsored building campaigns at Saint-Denis that sparked the new aesthetic. Constructional, formal, and theological ideas expressed in the architecture, monumental sculpture, and figurate glass of the windows in Suger's buildings quickly disseminated, developed, and resolved themselves into what we call today the Gothic style.[1] Scholars now agree that the three portals at Saint-Denis began the series of Early Gothic *portails royaux*. An innovation at Saint-Denis, twenty statue-columns, now lost, once flanked the portals. Representing mostly royal personages, such column-figures became the hallmark of Early Gothic portals. The less firmly dated but better preserved and more famous *portail royal* of the west facade at Chartres followed within the decade.

The sculptural programs on Gothic portals present in microcosm the Christian universe from the six days of Creation and the Fall of Man to the dreadful Day of Judgment. The building itself stood for the Heavenly Jerusalem, and the portals were the gates to paradise. During the Gothic period, such formulations of medieval thought attained great sophistication and complexity.

Yet the scholarly literature disputes whether the sculpture of the western portals at Saint-Denis culminated the High Romanesque period or, instead, merits the designation Gothic.[2] Although categorical definitions do not resolve the question, this study aims at clarifying distinctions between Romanesque and Early Gothic portal sculpture. In fact, the sculptural program of the western portals introduced concepts and aesthetic attitudes that distinguish it from High Romanesque portal programs. Even though many stylizations found in the figurate sculpture at Saint-Denis perpetuated motifs borrowed from the vocabulary of Romanesque drapery conventions, the artists ceased to use individual figures as vehicles for agitated surface-patterns. Such Romanesque designs yielded to arrangements stabilized by gravity and responsive to pose and gesture. To a marked degree the handling of the fabrics reflected weight and texture, and draperies increasingly suggested the volume and form of the body beneath. The figures evinced a new restraint in gesture and movement, and out of respect for the integrity of the human form, the Saint-Denis artists no longer allowed anatomically impossible poses. The anatomical verisimilitude of the nude figures indicated the artists' knowledge of and interest in musculature and bone structure—a reflection of the dawning of Gothic humanism, which brought with it a new respect for the individual. Displaying considerable sophistication, the Saint-Denis artists also increased the salience of the figures as the distance from the eye level of the viewer increased. Thus they began to correct for optical perspective and, by overlapping some of the forms, even achieved the illusion of depth.

Especially in the central portal (Plate I) a new calm and a didactic clarity of composition replaced the excitement and turbulence of Romanesque compositions. Appealing to the emotions, those turbulent, monumental representations of the Last Judgment deserve the epithet "epics of chaos."[3] But appealing instead to the intellect, the sculptural program of the three western portals at Saint-Denis presented a complex iconographical statement reflecting theological ideas then current in the Ile-de-France. Never in Romanesque portal programs do we find such complexities to challenge and inform the mind as those at Saint-Denis. Then, too, we no longer find the horror vacui characteristic of the crowded Romanesque compositions, where figures were often compressed to conform to the frames. Instead, negative spaces helped to organize interrelated themes and to emphasize the dominant ideas strategically located on the central axis. In the well-organized schema of the central portal, each part of the sculptural ensemble contributed to a unified statement. Indeed, when read in conjunction with the lateral portals, the interrelated themes acquired a significance and importance much greater than the sum of the parts. Unity emerges as one of the major characteristics of the Gothic style, whether architectural, sculptural, or iconographical. Thus, on compositional, formal, and iconographical grounds, the sculptural program of the central portal merits the designation Early Gothic rather than High Romanesque, even as we recognize the survival of Romanesque conventions that do not always live harmoniously with the new aesthetic concepts.

Innovations distinguishing the Saint-Denis portal from High Romanesque representations of the Last Judgment, such as those at Moissac (1115) and Autun (1130s), occurred in what one critic has called a "creative environment," achieved at Saint-Denis by the planning and patronage of Abbot Suger.[4] In 1091 Suger, aged ten and of humble origins, had been given by his parents to the abbey as an oblate. He was educated at the monastic school of Saint-Denis-de-l'Estrée—presumably for a short time in company with the heir to the French throne, the future Louis VI le Gros (1108–1137). Early on, Suger displayed the aptitude for administration and diplomacy that toward the end of his life earned him the post of coregent of France. He held the office from 1147 to 1149 during the absence of King Louis VII (1137–1180) on the ill-fated Second Crusade.[5] In two campaigns to enlarge and embellish the church, Suger achieved ambitions he had cherished even while a pupil. We know of his hopes and intentions from the record of his administration that he wrote "to save for the memory of posterity . . . those increments which the generous munificence of Almighty God had bestowed on the church" during his prelacy.[6]

As abbot and patron, Suger initiated campaigns to enlarge the church first to the west, then to the east. In the beginning, he left undisturbed the particularly venerated Carolingian nave, which he and his contemporaries believed had been built under the patronage of King Dagobert I (629–638). They had confused the eighth-century structure then extant with the seventh-century building, begun in circa 620. According to tradition, on the eve of the dedication ceremonies, Christ had descended miraculously to consecrate the nave of the earlier church.[7] After praising the "inestimable splendor" of the extant Carolingian structure, Suger stated that it was wanting only in size, for it could no longer accommodate the crowds that came on feast days to "seek the intercession of the saints."[8] Dramatizing the deficiency, he described how "no one among the countless thousands of people because of their very density could move a foot . . . [or do] anything but stand like a marble statue, stay benumbed or, as a last resort, scream." Women, he added, "squeezed by the mass of strong men as in a winepress, exhibited bloodless faces as in imagined death. . . . [and] cried out horribly as though in labor."[9]

Suger's westwork, or narthex, with its innovative triple-portal facade, was dedicated on 9 June 1140. To mark the occasion for posterity, Suger had the following words inscribed in copper-gilt letters on the facade:

> For the splendor of the church that has fostered and exalted him,
>
> Suger has labored for the splendor of the church.
>
> Giving thee a share of what is thine, O Martyr Denis,
>
> He prays to thee to pray that he may obtain a share of Paradise.
>
> The year was the One Thousand, One Hundred, and Fortieth
>
> Year of the Word when [this structure] was consecrated.[10]

Four years later ceremonies consecrating the altars in the new crypt and choir signaled the completion of Suger's eastern extension.[11]

The artists and workers whom Suger summoned for the campaigns probably came from regions he had visited in his extensive travels.[12] Besides bringing "many masters from different nations" to Saint-Denis to paint the glass for the windows, he gathered masons, carvers, metalworkers, mosaicists, jewelers, and enamel workers—skilled artists in every medium—who formed their ateliers on the site.[13] In such an international gathering, the work of each master and his assistants would have reflected the training and aesthetic preferences of their own region. But their exposure to the work of others must have catalyzed the experimentation and interchange of ideas visible in the sculpture of the central portal.

Inexplicably, in recounting the two campaigns, Suger never mentioned the sculptural program of the western portals—not even the stunning and influential innovation of statue-columns in the stepped embrasures flanking the three doorways. Yet he referred to the mosaic (now lost), "which, though contrary to modern custom," he had ordered for the tympanum of the left, or north, portal. He also quoted the inscription (also lost) that he had devised for the lintel of the central portal.[14] During his travels in Italy, he had doubtless seen the richly colored mosaics set in gold backgrounds on portals and in the apses and naves of churches and basilicas. But northern tastes probably would have found Suger's mosaic incongruous in a surround of stone carving.[15]

The brilliance and the gemlike refraction of light by the tesserae of mosaics would have had special appeal for Suger. He delighted in the sumptuous display of gold and gems embellishing altars and church furnishings and rationalized that delight as a way to rise from material things to the immaterial or spiritual—"de materialibus ad immaterialibus."[16] In the lines concluding the verses he composed for the gilded bronze doors of the central portal, he wrote:

> The dull mind rises to truth through that which is material
>
> And, in seeing this light, is resurrected from its former submersion.[17]

Then, referring to the gems of the altar furnishings, he rhapsodized:

> Thus, when—out of my delight in the beauty of the house of God—the loveliness
> of the many-colored gems has called me away from external cares, and worthy
> meditation has induced me to reflect, transferring that which is material to that
> which is immaterial, on the diversity of the sacred virtues: then it seems to me that
> I see myself dwelling, as it were, in some strange region of the universe which nei-
> ther exists entirely in the slime of earth nor entirely in the purity of Heaven; and
> that, by the grace of God, I can be transported from this inferior to that higher
> world in an anagogical manner.[18]

Much has been written linking Suger's anagogical method with the Christianized Neoplatonic view of the cosmos propounded in the *Celestial Hierarchy* and *Mystical Theology* of Dionysius the Pseudo-Areopagite, a sixth-century Near Eastern mystic.[19] In the ninth century, Abbot Hilduin (814–841) was the first to conflate St. Denis (in Latin, Sanctus Dionysius), the patron saint of the abbey, with Dionysius the Pseudo-Areopagite. The abbot also stated that the Pseudo-Areopagite and Dionysius the Athenian, whom St. Paul had converted to Christianity on the Areopagus in Athens (Acts 17:34), were one and the same.[20] Questioned only by Abelard in the twelfth century, the con-flation of the three was fully accepted, even though the disciple of St. Paul had lived in the first century, the patron saint of the abbey in the third, and the Pseudo-Areopagite in the sixth.[21]

St. Denis had been sent from Rome in the third century to Christianize Gaul. After enduring numerous tortures for steadfastly refusing to renounce the Christian faith and worship Roman gods, he suffered martyrdom in 251 by order of the Roman consul Fescinius (Siscinnius). The execution took place in the vil-lage of Catulliacum, the present faubourg of Saint-Denis. Through the centuries those documentable facts were embellished until the fully developed legend of the saint placed his martyrdom in Paris on Montmartre, in the company of two legendary and sainted companions, Rusticus and Eleutherius.[22] According to the legend, the night before the execution Christ himself administered the Eucharist to the three prisoners. After the execution by Roman soldiers, St. Denis is said to have picked up his severed head and, carrying it before him, walked due north to Catulliacum, thus choosing his place of burial. The legend states that as he made that miraculous walk, his lips chanted psalms in praise of the Lord.

Excavations and early texts attest to three, possibly four, earlier structures erected successively on the site of the saint's grave. Transcribed in the sixth century, the earliest known text on the martyrdom of St. Denis tells how a pious woman named Catulla erected a mausoleum above the saint's tomb.[23] Vestiges of Gallo-Roman masonry beneath the existing church suggest that a second- or third-century structure once existed near his grave.[24] Possibly those huge reused blocks came from the mausoleum first erected above his burial place.[25] The Life of Ste. Geneviève, the patron saint of Paris (d. ca. 512), which was written shortly after her death or in circa 520, never mentions a mausoleum or shrine, but according to her biographer the tomb was in a "terrible and fearful" place.[26] The first church documented by Crosby's excavations and dated to circa 475 was probably the one Ste. Geneviève persuaded the bishops of Paris to build in honor of St. Denis.[27] Excavations indicate that it was hardly more than a chapel. Then, under the patronage of Dagobert I, the chapel built on the urging of Ste. Geneviève was enlarged at the east and west to more than double the original size.[28] By the twelfth century, because of his lavish patronage of the building campaign, his costly gifts, and the royal privileges he granted the abbey, Dagobert was incorrectly credited by Suger and his contemporaries as the founder.[29] Around 755, Pepin the Short, king of the Franks (751–768), began the next church on the site, the one still extant in Suger's time. Completed by his son Charlemagne (768–814), the church was dedicated in 775 in the presence of the king and his court. But by the twelfth century, according to Suger, the building had aged to the point of "impending ruin in some places."[30]

Determining first to renovate the Carolingian nave,[31] and then to enlarge and embellish the church, Suger also successfully strove to strengthen the power and authority of the French monarchy. Indeed, he saw the two goals as synonymous and believed that achieving both would reinforce the historical association of the monarchy and abbey in the eyes of his contemporaries.

From the time of Dagobert's father, Clothaire II (d. ca. 629), French monarchs had venerated St. Denis as their particular patron and protector, and, by extension, he became recognized as the patron saint of all France.[32] Legends of posthumous miracles occurring at the saint's shrine further emphasized St. Denis's role as protector of the monarchy.[33] The first known royal burials at Saint-Denis took place early in the Merovingian period; then from 987 on, with three exceptions, all kings and queens of France chose to be buried there.[34] Through the centuries, munificent royal gifts, grants, and privileges fostered the royal association and enriched the abbey until it became in name as well as in fact "the Royal Abbey of Saint-Denis."[35]

Damage to the church over time unquestionably modified and depleted the architecture, sculpture, and ornament of Suger's campaigns. The portals could scarcely have escaped some mutilation in the fifteenth century during the Hundred Years' War, when the city and abbey were repeatedly assaulted and captured. Again in 1567, toward the end of the Wars of Religion, the abbey was the center of conflict and pillaging by the Huguenots.[36] Although no documents record the damage to the portals during those conflicts, the alterations and repairs undertaken in 1770 and 1771 attest to the deteriorated state of some of the sculpture. More than a restoration, the modifications forever altered the appearance of the three portals.

Most of the information about the work done in 1770 and 1771 comes from the eighteenth-century record of events at the abbey kept by Ferdinand-Albert Gautier, the organist of the church in the last decades of the century.[37] The central portal was enlarged to accommodate the royal catafalque and the elaborate canopies used in funerals and other ceremonial processions. To that end the trumeau figure depicting St. Denis as a bishop, which had divided the central portal, was eliminated, and at the same time the lintel bearing Suger's inscription was probably removed and replaced. The monks had also ordered the dismounting of the twenty statue-columns in the embrasures of the three doorways, thereby robbing them of their most impressive attributes.[38] But we know from a marginal note in a nineteenth-century document that the statues were removed because of their ruined condition.[39]

Fortunately, earlier in the eighteenth century, Antoine Benoît had made drawings of all the statue-columns, the trumeau figure of St. Denis, and two column-figures from the cloister. When Bernard de Montfaucon published

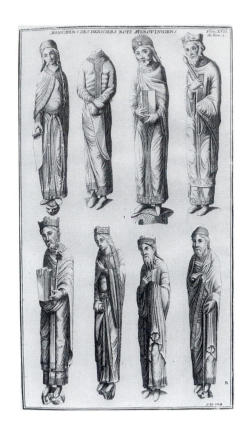

FIG. 1. Lost statue-columns of the central portal. Drawing by Antoine Benoît. After Montfaucon 1 [1729], pl. XVII

engravings of the drawings in 1729, he identified the portal figures as statues of the kings and queens of the Merovingian dynasty.[40] Because he misunderstood their significance, we have a record of the lost statues (Fig. 1). We now know that they depicted not the early rulers of France but the ancestors and precursors of Christ—the kings and prophets of the Old Testament.[41] One critic stated that Montfaucon had reproduced the drawings "tant bien que mal."[42] Yet the engravings, together with Benoît's original drawings, have been used convincingly to identify the five surviving heads from the lost statue-columns as well as one of the figures from the cloister.[43]

The alterations of 1770–1771 also affected the jambs of all three portals. Gautier's account of the work has been misleading. Although he documented the chapter's wish to enlarge the central entrance, he failed to add that in the course of the alterations some of the masonry of the jambs had been dismantled and reassembled and the sculptures somewhat restored.[44] The more detailed notes kept by Ferdinand François, baron de Guilhermy, on work in progress on the portals in 1839–1840 nourished the generally held misconception that the jamb sculptures, particularly those of the lateral portals, had survived relatively unscathed and unrestored until the nineteenth century.[45] Possibly the jambs of the left and right portals were taken down and remounted in 1770–1771, but certainly their sculptures—the Signs of the Zodiac on the left portal and the

Labors of the Months on the right—were sensitively restored at that time.[46] Predictably, those smaller and quite delicate jamb carvings had been as vulnerable to the assaults of time, weather, and wars as the large-scale statue-columns in the adjacent embrasures.

Saint-Denis, the royal abbey and repository of the royal regalia, became the particularly hated target of the French Revolution. In 1793 the devastation began. To commemorate the anniversary of the downfall of the monarchy, the national committee ordered the destruction of the royal tombs and all vestiges of memorials to the monarchs of France and their families. Already begun in 1791, the violation of tombs gained momentum. After the royal tombs in the choir had been emptied, the central crypt, or *caveau royal,* of the Bourbon dynasty was breached and the tombs opened. The remains of the disinterred royalty were then thrown pell-mell into ditches in the cemetery outside the north transept and covered with quicklime. Gautier commented on the terrible stench from recent burials.[47] Not until October 1793 did the Parisian mobs arrive in the faubourg to storm the basilica. Although no documents record their damage to the abbey, surely we can blame the inflamed mobs for the systematic mutilation of the sculpture of the western portals.[48] Doubtless unaware that the figures in the archivolts of the central portal were the elders of the Apocalypse, the revolutionary zealots knocked off their crowned heads as well as those of most other figures in the three portals.[49]

In the ensuing months, the church, stripped of its golden altar frontals, costly altar furnishings, royal regalia, and centuries of accumulated treasures, served first as a temple for the Cult of Reason and subsequently as a granary. By April 1794 the building had become uninhabitable. In that year the three sets of bronze doors in the western portals went to the mint to be melted down.[50] The roof had been stripped of its lead sheathing—a depredation that exposed the building to the elements—and many of the dismantled royal tombs went piece by piece to the depot of the Petits Augustins in Paris to be inaccurately reassembled by Alexandre Lenoir and put on exhibition in his Musée des Monuments français.[51] Fortunately, a proposal to bombard the facade and knock down the spire was voted down on the grounds that the spire might in some circumstances serve as an observation point.[52] A decision to dismantle the vaults of the nave and build a cover over the lower stories was never implemented, but the prospect emboldened Lenoir to strip the north transept portal

9

of its statue-columns and dismount other architectural ornament, sculpture, and the glass of the windows for display in his museum.

Thus despoiled, Saint-Denis was in danger of falling into ruin. Describing the deserted and derelict abbey, one observer wrote, "The birds make their passage through it, grass grows on the broken altars. Instead of the sung litanies of the dead that once echoed under its vaults, one hears only drops of rain that fall on the open roof, the tumble of stones breaking off from the ruined walls, or the clock resounding in the empty tombs and devastated crypts."[53]

Saved from complete destruction in the early nineteenth century,[54] the once-royal abbey was next subjected to a mindless reconstruction, ordered by Napoleon in 1806. Hoping to enhance his imperial dignity by associating himself with the pantheon of the French monarchy, Napoleon determined to repossess the abbey as an imperial mausoleum for his dynasty. One of the initial works of the reconstruction—the only one affecting the western portals—involved the raising of the level of the pavement of the western bays and of the parterre in front of the portals.[55] Stunting the proportions of the portals, those two alterations persist to this day (compare Figs. 2 and 3).[56] Reroofing the structure and reglazing the windows closed out the elements. But not confined to reclaiming the abbey from wind and weather and reestablishing the Catholic cult, Napoleon's orders to embellish the church resulted in alterations that threatened the stability of the building. As the transformation of the interior of the abbey progressed in accordance with the tastes of the Empire period, the shaving of piers and bases prior to facing them with black marble, the sapping of supports in the crypt, and the paring of all the exterior mural surfaces to refurbish them put the building in dangerous disequilibrium. Expenditures for sculptures and the other imperial embellishments greatly exceeded the allotted funds. Although some of the sculptural works were abandoned unfinished, pretentious marble and limestone groups of figures ordered as memorials to the earlier dynasties still gather dust in chapels of the crypt.

Three successive architects-in-chief from 1805 to 1845 squandered millions of francs in compromising the twelfth- and thirteenth-century building and its ornament.[57] Following the orders of Napoleon or the whims of the restored Bourbons, each architect left a heavy-handed imprint on the architecture and ornament of the church.

10

CHAPTER 2

NINETEENTH-CENTURY
RESTORATIONS

In 1846 the archaeologist Didron, *aîné*, wrote a diatribe against the restorations effected under the direction of François Debret (1813–1846). Concluding that it would be impossible to spoil Saint-Denis any further, Didron lamented: "Le mal est fait, et parfait." To restore Saint-Denis when only wars and revolutions had left their mark on the monument would have been possible, he continued, though not easy. But to reclaim the church in 1846, after seven million francs had been spent systematically spoiling it, would be a task beyond the capabilities of archaeology.[1]

Until 1837, the beginning of Debret's final decade as architect-in-chief, the western portals had escaped a nineteenth-century restoration. As work on the building neared completion, Debret proposed the restoration of the sculpture—a project that appalled some but by no means all of his contemporaries. In the same year a bolt of lightning struck the north tower, thereby providing him with an excuse to restore the entire facade.[2] Although the electrical storm did not affect the portals, the earlier damage to the sculpture seemed to justify its repair. Debret commissioned the well-known sculptor Joseph-Sylvestre Brun, who from 1837 to 1839 worked single-handedly to restore the figurate sculpture of the three portals;[3] accounts show assistants receiving payment only for carving foliate ornament.[4] After assaults on the portals by time and wars, Brun's work proved the final indignity. In Didron's estimation, the restoration had created a "façade défigurée, dépourvue à tout jamais d'intérêt historique, et fort laide d'ailleurs."[5]

Didron used the publication *Annales archéologiques,* a journal he had founded, as the vehicle to alert the world to the incalculable damage that French monuments and sculpture were suffering in the name of restoration. Using the work at Saint-Denis as the tragic example, he and his collaborator,

Guilhermy, filled pages describing the atrocities committed under Debret's direction.[6] By exposing what he called the acts of vandalism and "le massacre de Saint-Denis,"[7] especially with respect to the restored portals, together they hoped to save the sculpture of other treasured monuments from a similar fate.[8]

Over the years, the Administration of Public Works had given Debret enthusiastic approval for everything he proposed and from 1830 on had supplied almost limitless funding. But his restoration of the facade caused such a stir that an official investigation followed, with a full report to the minister of the interior itemizing the egregious mistakes.[9] Debret replied in detail to the charges against him.[10] Yet opinion proved so divided that officials of the Académie des Beaux-Arts were called in to judge the matter.[11] To Didron's dismay, the officials exonerated their colleague, suppressed the critical report, and Debret continued in his post at Saint-Denis. But his shocking ineptitude soon became evident. He had rebuilt the damaged spire with stone of a greater weight than the original. The new spire put such an overload on the supporting structure that its stability was threatened, and fissures opened up across the facade that invaded the stones of the tympana. Finally Debret was relieved of his post, but with a promotion.[12] The post of architect-in-chief at Saint-Denis was offered first to one M. Duban, who accepted but then withdrew.[13] In 1846, the young architect Eugène Viollet-le-Duc assumed responsibility for Saint-Denis with the intention of restoring the abbey as far as possible to its original state. He began by stabilizing the portions of the building that Debret had left in jeopardy.[14]

Beginning in the 1790s, records of public works were preserved by the national government.[15] Although far from complete, they help to reconstruct the history of the nineteenth-century restorations. Yet because of uncertainties about what had survived untouched from the twelfth century, historians of art have slighted the sculpture of the west facade in discussions of Early Gothic sculpture in the Ile-de-France. Misunderstandings of the written reports and of the archaeological evidence marred their conclusions concerning the portal ensemble. Whether critics dismissed the sculptures as completely restored but accepted the iconography as valid, all had apparently based their judgments on an examination made from ground level.[16]

Since the restorations under Debret, no significant alterations have affected the sculpture of the western portals.[17] The nineteenth-century work remains the critical problem in any evaluation of the style and iconography of the portal ensemble. Unfortunately, the location of the royal abbey in a Parisian suburb destined to become an important industrial center has magnified the problems in many ways. As early as the 1860s more than forty-five industries began to saturate the air with chemical effluents.[18] The pollution increased as the twentieth century advanced, until all exterior surfaces of the church became corroded and soiled.[19] The decay and encrustation affected not only the surfaces of the surviving original work, but also those of the restoration—a shared condition confusing at first even to the practiced eye.

Unsound practices employed in the restoration had put some of the surviving sculptures at risk. In deference to their delicate condition the portals were not touched in the campaign of the early 1970s to clean the west facade. Yet while the south side of the west facade lay behind scaffolding covered with green baize, three roundels containing the Labors of the Months on the right jamb of the right portal were cleaned with water and sand. The pressure used was strong enough to remove the protective coating of mastic (applied as a liquid, which then hardened) as well as the grime. With those exceptions, the sculptures on all three portals remain darkened with grime, and many of them are still covered with mastic.[20]

Although disagreeing in details, the two recent attempts to ascertain the extent of damage and repairs to the portals both pointed to the need for a complete examination of the sculpture.[21] As the only way to eliminate uncertainties created by the restoration, an archaeological study of the sculpture at close quarters was begun in 1968 to identify all unspoiled twelfth-century carving. Satisfactory examination of the tympana and archivolts of the doorways was possible only from scaffolding.

The results presented in this volume are based on a meticulous examination of all carved surfaces under magnification.[22] Since layers of soot and encrustations of grime masking the carved surfaces proved a major obstacle to close observation, permission was granted to dust them lightly with a toothbrush, as needed. The brushing—definitely not a cleaning—made it possible to follow the course of mortar joints attaching the nineteenth-century carved insets, which were often partially concealed by dirt, and to expose grainy surfaces where the twelfth-century carving had been recut.

Sanding and recutting had frequently eliminated all or most of the patina of age that had survived intact on unretouched surfaces. Identifying all insets

13

and recutting required painstaking and repeated inspections of each carved figure under different lighting conditions. At times the light on an overcast day
proved more revealing than the dazzling light of the afternoon sun on the
west facade. Often the light at noon, just before the sun rounded the south
tower, disclosed restorations not visible under other lighting conditions. The
examination established which areas had been recut and which consisted of
carved replacements of lost elements, and achieved its purpose by authenticating areas of well-preserved twelfth-century carving untouched by the
restorer's chisel.

Determination of the extent of the damages, losses, and restorations to the
sculpture provides the essential prelude to any consideration of iconography
and style. As Erwin Panofsky once wrote, "Archaeological research is blind and
empty without aesthetic re-creation; and aesthetic re-creation is irrational and
often misguided, without archaeological research."[23] In effect, the archaeological
examination allows us to rediscover the style of the twelfth-century carvers of
the central portal and also the iconographical intentions of those who formu-
lated the portal program. With that knowledge, the portal can resume its
rightful place in discussions of the influences upon and formation of the Early
Gothic style in the Ile-de-France.[24]

Consistent with the lack of precise information about restorations to the
western portals, information about their prerestoration appearance also proved
inconclusive. For example, the earliest known drawing of the portals, a small-
scale sketch of the entire facade made by Vincenzo Scamozzi in 1600, shows the
original lofty proportions of the doorways prior to the raising of the pavement
in 1806, as does the one made in 1700 by Martellange (Fig. 2). The latter also
indicates the trumeau of the central portal still in situ, and both sketches suggest
that none of the portals had a lintel of any significant height. Yet despite those
visual documents, the debate whether or not the portals originally had lintels
with carved decoration has continued.[25]

Unfortunately, in both drawings the details of the portal sculpture proved
too sketchy to be useful.[26] Although prerestoration nineteenth-century drawings
such as the one signed by Cellérier and Legrand (Fig. 3) provide more information than the earlier two, the architects did not draw the sculpture to scale,
and their drawings contain obvious inaccuracies (Fig. 4). *Attachements* signed
by Debret in 1838 presumably should show us exactly what was restored and

FIG. 2.   West facade.
Drawing by Martellange
of 1700, showing portals
before the level of the
pavement was raised.
Paris, Archives des
Monuments historiques

FIG. 3.   West facade.
Drawing by Cellérier and
Legrand, ca. 1815, after the
raising of the pavement.
Album Debret, Paris,
Archives des Monuments
historiques

FIG. 4.   Tympanum of the
central portal. Detail of
drawing by Cellérier and
Legrand (Fig. 3), ca. 1815

FIG. 5. *Attachement* show-
ing reparations to the cen-
tral portal proposed by
Debret, 1840. Album
Debret, Paris, Archives des
Monuments historiques

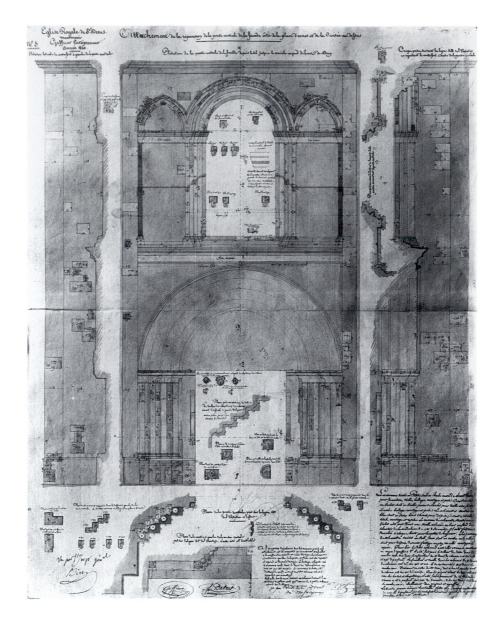

what remained untouched (Fig. 5). But in many instances, because the details
do not correspond to what exists today, the *attachements* evidently represented Debret's intentions rather than his actual accomplishments.[27] As for written evidence, Guilhermy's record of the restorations to the portals based on his
observations made in the course of the work have proved quite accurate, but not
sufficiently detailed. Yet some of his conclusions about preexisting arrangements
as well as some of his iconographical interpretations do not agree with the surviving evidence.

The precise information accumulated from the scaffolding is presented
here in diagrams which are superimposed on photographs. They identify all
untouched or surviving twelfth-century carving, every nineteenth-century
inset and repair, and all recut or retouched surfaces.[28] This study focuses on the

sculptural decoration of the central portal; iconographical and stylistic observations accompany the validation of twelfth-century sculptural details.[29]
Furthermore, awareness of different stylistic and aesthetic preferences mani-
fested in the unrestored portions of the figures allows the identification of
the distinct styles of three twelfth-century artists who worked on the portal,
namely, the Master of the Apostles, the Master of the Tympanum Angels, and
the Master of the Elders. In effect, the purpose of the archaeological examination is realized with the rediscovery of the twelfth-century styles and in the verification of iconographical details.

An understanding of how the twelfth-century portal was constructed
proved essential in order to distinguish the nineteenth-century restorations from
the original work. A number of perplexing irregularities in the masonry of the
lower portions of the portal led to a careful study of the construction of the
entire doorway and the adjacent buttresses of the facade (Figs. 6a–b, and
Plates I, Xa, and XIa). Except where interrupted by repairs, the bottom or first
four beds of masonry are continuous across the buttresses and both embrasures
of the portal.[30] That linkage or bonding of the masonry between the buttresses
and the portal structures ceases on both sides at the fifth bed of masonry and
begins again in the spandrels between the buttresses and the archivolts, above
the level of the capitals. The lack of linkage indicates that the decorated portions
of the portal with which we are concerned were built as independent entities
and apparently were inserted into the mural masonry of the west facade. The
quality of limestone used for the portal sculpture has a much finer grain than
that of the mural masonry. Emphasizing the structural independence or dif-
ferentiation, the blocks of limestone in the doorways measure 29.5 cm. high and
lie in regular horizontal beds, whereas the masonry of the buttresses and of the
interior walls of the western bays—all part of the same campaign of building—
has beds of stone that vary from 12 to 48 cm. in height. The uniformity of the
portal masonry provided an objective control for detection of restorations in the
decoration of the jambs. Stones that disrupt or are at variance with the regular
masonry must be regarded as inserts into or changes within the original
construction.[31]

The tympanum was carved from two large, originally rectangular stones
shaped to form a hemicycle. Pressures exerted on those blocks caused extensive
irregular fractures that must have endangered the solidity of the tympanum and

17

FIG. 6a. Central portal,
left jamb

required unusual procedures to strengthen and support it.[32] Because the fractures continued into the narrow lintel stone, it could not adequately support the tympanum. To remedy this condition, an iron band, now functioning as the lintel, was inserted under the lintel stone. Large plaques of stone were also bolted to the back, or interior face, of the entire tympanum, presumably to stabilize it.[33]

Knowledge of the techniques and materials of the nineteenth-century restorers and an understanding of the various ways they could manipulate them was a prerequisite for recognizing their work. Because of the accidental and essentially irrational character of most of the damage, only minute examination of every figure could determine the type and extent of its restoration.[34] Fractures and decay of stone along masonry joints constituted usual areas for repairs. Projecting elements such as heads, hands, and accompanying attributes naturally suffered more than the less salient carved surfaces. To repair the heaviest damages and remedy major losses, the restorers depended primarily on newly carved insets, which they secured with metal dowels as well as mortar. A look at the diagrams (Plates IIb–XIb) shows recutting as the primary method for eliminating both major and minor mutilation. Although occasionally heavy enough to cause deformation, some of the recutting barely skinned the surface. For other repairs, the restorer drew on a reservoir of supplementary techniques involving such materials as mastic, mortar, cement, and a composite or manufactured stone as well as a gessolike material resembling terra cotta, and a liquid preservative, or mastic, that coated surfaces and gave them a shiny, uniform appearance.

Although each material seemed to have had a primary function, convenience often dictated some interchanges. Three distinctive types of mortar and a pure white cement occur throughout the portal. Those substances were used to close fractures, bind insets, and restore the masonry. The fine-grained white cement provides reinforcement for both freestanding twelfth-century sculptural elements and nineteenth-century insets. Only occasionally does it actually form the joint for an inset. As a binder, it apparently lacked the durability of the buff-colored mortar, the preferred material for attaching insets. Sometimes used lavishly in a masonry joint or as remedy for a clumsily fitting inset, the buff-colored mortar also occurs in beautifully executed hairline joinings. Their perfect condition in some of the most exposed locations testifies to the strength and endurance of the material.[35] A more granular grayish mortar

FIG. 6b.   Central portal, right jamb

proved most effective in closing eroded and separated masonry joints. It was also used for minor patching where the damaged area seemed too small for a carved stone inset. Occasionally that mortar fills out a small break along the edge of a garment or on the frame of a musical instrument—minor repairs of the type usually reserved for mastic. The third type of mortar, a granular mixture compounded with reddish sand, occurs exclusively in repairs of voussoirs and moldings, and on the background planes, never in the sculpture proper. That material has weathered very badly and continues to crumble and fall away. A fine-grained gessolike substance with a glossy surface repairs whole sections of the foliate rinceau to the left of the Wise Virgins on the left jamb and also reconstitutes a portion of the acanthus motif ornamenting the molding of the tympanum on the left side, behind the head of the trumpeting angel.[36] In a few instances, as substitution for one of the mortars, the material spreads over small sections of a fracture or over the joint of a badly fitting inset. Composite manufactured stone occurs only in the replacements of the jamb-colonnettes. Cast from molds made from the originals, those decorative colonnettes of *pierre factice* now occupy the recessed angles of the jambs of all three portals.[37]

Two types of mastic, now a dark gray approaching black, provided a suitable substance for delicate surface repairs. In the lintel zone of the tympanum, dribbles of mastic on the lid and front surface of the first sarcophagus on the left indicate that here the substance was applied in a liquid state (see no. 11, Plate IIIa, and the schema preceding Plate I that locates and identifies each figure). Used in that form over limited areas, the mastic smooths over abrasions or pitting. In some instances the liquid mastic seems to provide a protective coating, a thin shell-like crust, through which even the most delicate modeling of the original sculpture emerges. When tapped lightly, those resurfaced areas respond with a dry, metallic click.[38] That type of coating occurs primarily on the jamb sculpture of all three portals, as well as in the lintel zone of the central doorway. The initial use of the liquid mastic presumably dates from the alterations of 1770 and 1771.[39] When making surface repairs in the archivolts and higher zones of the tympanum, the nineteenth-century restorer applied mastic in a less viscous and more malleable form that did not harden into a brittle skin. He used it primarily to smooth over and fill out nicks, chips, and other superficial damage, and to repair ornamental borders and broken ridges of folds in the drapery. Occasionally the buff-colored mortar substitutes for mastic in such minor surface repairs.

In the jambs and archivolts, mortar often sufficed to point up the masonry joints. But when deterioration had progressed too far, particularly when the eroded joint impinged on one of the figures, the crumbling edges were cut away in preparation for insertions of *couvres-joints*. Those bands of nineteenth-century stone either lie along or interrupt the original masonry joint, and the repair generally caused some distortion to both drapery and figure (Plates Xb and XIb).

The limestone used for insets in the nineteenth-century work approached the creamy, fine-grained twelfth-century limestone in quality but appears slightly yellower and coarser to the eye than the original. The broken surfaces, newly revealed by recent losses of both old and new carving, are still clean and therefore clearly show the differences in color and grain. The weathered surfaces of both the old and new stone also present contrasts in color and in texture that helped to distinguish them. As the carved surfaces of the restoration stone became coated and ingrained with industrial dirt, the larger insets acquired a uniform cold monotonic gray color quite distinct from the more variegated gray hues of the weathered twelfth-century stone. Warmed by tones of yellowish buff, the original stone has attained a mellow glow. Age and weather have crackled and pitted its surface or skin, now dappled with buff-colored specks in varying concentrations. The variegated aspect of the skin, or patina of age, resulted from minerals in the stone that were carried to the surface as the newly quarried stone dried. Aging of the patina created the effect resembling craquelure. In comparison, the nineteenth-century stone appears smooth. Identification of the two stones depended equally on those differences in texture and color that emerged readily after a light brushing with a toothbrush had disturbed the overlay of soot and dust.

Depending on its thoroughness, recutting and sanding of the old stone either removed or diminished the encrustation and the characteristic buff-colored dappling. A white powder, mingling with and dissipating in clouds of soot, invariably rose from the recut surfaces as they were brushed. The powdering suggests that recut and sanded areas were primed with a substance like plaster of Paris or gesso as a preparation for overpainting intended to harmonize the newly cut surfaces with the original, unspoiled carving. The restorer's

FIG. 7. Central portal, socle. Detail of Gate to Paradise, first archivolt, left

concern for the final effect required a uniform hue for the finished work. In addition, the recut stone often retains telling striations representing tooth-marks of the nineteenth-century chisel. The discordant sharpness of recut details contrasts with the finely drawn details of the original carving, now somewhat muted by the pitting and encrustation of age (Fig. 7). The crackled surface of the pristine twelfth-century stone also provided a more retentive base for the deposits of soot, which adhered less well to the smoother surfaces of the recut or nineteenth-century stone. In the outer archivolts, however, weathering has accelerated the accumulation of all deposits and encrustation to a point where it is difficult to recognize insets and distinguish between unretouched and recut surfaces.

Where damage was severe, the surgery required to insert a newly carved element unfortunately caused additional destruction and loss of twelfth-century carving. A good joining for an inset necessitated the elimination of jagged stumps and all irregular surfaces along the old breaks. In the archivolts, the restorers usually achieved the optimal flat surface by cutting back to the nearest joint, which offered a structural camouflage for the repair. With few exceptions, the joints of the voussoirs coincide with the base of the neck or collar line. Identification of those insets therefore depended on the clearly visible stylistic anomalies and the textural and color differences between the old and new stone. The tympanum had no such joints to determine or limit the extent of the incursion into the old stone or to facilitate the preparation of good surfaces to receive insets replacing the heads. In the tympanum, most of the joinings for the heads lie partially concealed by the edge of a collar, striations of the hair, or a

21

fold of drapery. The cutting away of figures was usually kept to a minimum. Nevertheless, in several instances the figures appear to have been restored in a manner that facilitated the repairs at the expense of some of the original work (see Apostles nos. 28 and 31, Plate IVb). If possible, the restorer tried to hide joinings by making them coincide with the contours of the replaced member, whether an arm, a hand, a foot, or an attribute (see no. 31, Plate IVb). When the random nature of the damage did not allow this concealment, scattered insets create a patchwork across the figure (see no. 27, Plate IIIb).

The use of metal dowels to secure most insets has caused postrestoration fractures in both the original and the nineteenth-century stone, as well as numerous losses that clearly reveal the techniques used to attach the repair. Because of their small scale, the figures of the Resurrected Dead of the lintel zone have suffered especially severe attrition. On the right, in the second sarcophagus from the center, the figure to the right of the bishop has lost the two insets that restored his right shoulder and head (no. 16b, Fig. 8). The remaining stump of twelfth-century stone shows not only two dowel scars but also heavy patches of white mortar—vestiges of reinforcing fill never intended to be seen from the front. The smoothed surfaces that were prepared to receive the insets are visible on the right shoulder and at chin level. Apparently owing to seasonal temperature changes, expansion and contraction of the two metal dowels caused the twelfth-century stone to split and, in time, to fall away. Because the dowels were inserted at the same angle and on nearly the same plane, their movement destroyed portions of the outer surfaces of the original upper torso, the right arm almost to the wrist, and the left forearm and hand. Frequently a figure required more than one inset, each doweled from a different angle (nos. 11b, 13c, and 17b, Plates IIIb and IVb). But the old stone suffered the greatest stress when both dowels were located at the same level and on approximately the same plane.

In the small figures, the stone of the nineteenth-century insets withstood the expansion and contraction of the dowels no better than the twelfth-century stone. The resulting pressures have fractured some of the restorations and caused sections of the insets to fall away. Those losses always reveal either dowels or their scars as well as the surfaces of the twelfth-century stone cut and dressed to receive the missing portion of the inset. Unfortunately, new fractures now threaten additional losses of both old and new stone.

FIG. 8. Detail of frieze of the Resurrected Dead, lintel zone, right, no. 16b

Two figures provide evidence of a last-minute change of mind about procedures in the restoration. After outlining an area for excision with an incised line, the restorer decided against an inset and instead recut the damaged surface. Although recutting has eliminated all traces of mutilation, the incisions remain clearly visible across the recut thumbs of the Deity in the representation of the Trinity (no. XVIII, Plate Vb), and around the heavily recut face of the figure of the Blessed in the portal of the Heavenly City (no. VI, Plate VIb).

The final comments on the attrition of nineteenth-century repairs concern their erosion. Besides some loss of the cement and mortar that fill fractures, point up masonry joints, and repair the surface planes of the voussoirs, scattered flakes of eroded mastic indicate that many mastic repairs have peeled and dropped off, revealing the original surfaces, unrecut but pitted and scarred. That phenomenon probably explains why some of the current observations are at variance with those made several decades ago. In noting the reworking of draperies, the earlier observers frequently failed to specify whether recutting, mastic, or mortar had been employed. Since many areas once identified as "retouched" now reveal unrestored and often somewhat abraded twelfth-century surfaces, one suspects that the crust of mastic may have fallen away because of weathering in conditions of ever-increasing air pollution.

During the examination of the sculpture, evidence accumulated to suggest a scattering of minor alterations made in this century. Unfortunately no records

23

FIG. 9. Twelfth-century hands. Detail of Apostle no. 30, tympanum, right

were kept detailing the work done or noting the persons or agency involved. Photographs taken in 1935 and 1947 record a number of carved elements that had disappeared by 1968. One of the 1935 photographs shows irregular projections of stone flanking the lower half of the head of the second Apostle on Christ's left (no. 29, Plate IVa).[40] The perspective of the photograph, slightly above and to the right of the head, made the rough stone fragments appear to rise from behind the Apostle's shoulders. Because of the location, the projections cannot be construed as vestiges or stumps of original heads. Pictured in a 1947 photograph, another unidentifiable carved fragment located between the third and fourth Apostles on Christ's left (nos. 30 and 31) was once mistaken for the left arm of Apostle no. 30 (Plate IVa). Since the fragment could not be reconciled with the pose and gestures of the figure, the beautifully preserved, folded, twelfth-century hands of the Apostle were dismissed as nineteenth-century fabrications (Fig. 9). We cannot ascertain from the photographs whether that unidentifiable carved element (also visible in earlier photographs) was associated in any way with the remnants already mentioned.

Another loss, a lesser one, involved a rectangular fragment that projected from the surface plane below the crook of the right wing of the angel on Christ's left, upper tympanum zone (no. IV, Plate IId). The location suggests that the missing stump probably was carved of a piece with the angel's twelfth-century head and linked it to the upper tympanum stone. The removal of all those fragments seems to represent an effort to tidy the tympanum. To judge from the photographs, all surfaces exposed after the fragments were chiseled away were painted gray to achieve a uniform appearance. Possibly the painting coincided with the removal of the fragments. As mentioned elsewhere, surfaces exposed since then by losses of stone still retain either the yellowish color of restoration stone or the creamier shades of the twelfth-century stone.

Study of the sculpture at very close quarters quickly revealed a great variation in the quality of the restorations.[41] The differences pertain not only to the carving of the insets and the felicity of the joinings but also to the recutting and to other minor surface repairs. The work ranges from the crudely carved and clumsy inset that completes the lower half of the figure of the Wise Virgin in the lintel zone of the tympanum, far left (no. 5, Plate IIIb), to the barely visible mortar filling Christ's wound (no. I, Plate IIb), as well as to the joint of an unobtrusive inset replacing the ear of the Lamb in the center of the third archivolt (no. XVIII, Plate Vb). Decay of the stone and the crust formed by industrial soot compounded the difficulties in locating such skillful insets, whereas the unfortunate facial style of the nineteenth-century heads, so blatantly incompatible with the twelfth-century sculpture, instantly proclaimed their modernity even in the most heavily eroded figures.

Assistance in pinpointing inserted repairs came not only from contrasts in the quality of the carving, stylistic incongruities, and the visible differences in surface colors and textures, but also from formal confusions such as unconvincing drapery arrangements or perplexing and inexplicit poses. For example, the awkward pose and stylistically discordant drapery over the right leg of the third Apostle from the left (no. 23, Plate IIIa–b), clearly identified a problem area. Visually incongruous forms coextensive with a nineteenth-century inset were often attended by minor recutting of adjacent surfaces. Drastic recutting in severely damaged areas occasionally provided equally disturbing effects. Patriarch C, on the far left in the lowest tier of the fourth archivolt (Plate VIa–b), and patriarch H, third archivolt, left, third tier (Plate VIIa–b), contain excellent examples of distortions created by recutting. The lower left portion of the former must have suffered considerable damage along the left side. The inset along the hem and the severe cutting-back of the leg, especially around the knee, and of the attendant drapery, not only created an anatomical aberration but also may have altered the pose. The original arrangement probably approximated that of patriarch G (Plate VIIa), who sits with his right leg crossed over his left, and with his feet, although nearly parallel, also crossed. Eliminating the crossed legs of patriarch C may have enabled the restorer to minimize the size of the inset, but in so doing, he reduced the forward projection of the legs and sacrificed the forms beneath the drapery—forms strongly evoked in the better-preserved twelfth-century figures. Recutting has also noticeably changed the proportions of the lower half of patriarch H (Plate VIIa–b), and has both distorted and modified the drapery arrangement, especially from the knee down on the right side. In addition, the drastic recutting of his bench has destroyed its orthogonal perspective. The adjacent surface planes of the voussoirs appear cut back, and heavy recutting eliminated some of the foliage forming the footrest directly below. In short, the illegibility of a pose, of drapery, or of form and anatomy invariably bespeaks the hand of the restorer rather than the ineptness of the original design.

CHAPTER 3

THE GREAT TYMPANUM
OF THE CENTRAL PORTAL

THE FIGURE OF CHRIST

The massive figure of Christ (no. I, Plate IIa), one of the more controversial and generally disparaged sculptures at Saint-Denis, dominates the portal. Cut from the two great twelfth-century stones that form the tympanum, and projecting in high relief, this central figure extends across all three zones. The horizontal joint between the two stones bisects Christ's torso—a line now emphasized by the heavy and distorting overlay of nineteenth-century mortar fill. The drapery covering Christ's body consists primarily of a tunic and a loosely arranged mantle. But the degree of overlapping and the heavy, stylized fold curving from under the right shoulder across the abdomen can only be described as arbitrary. Despite the extensive recutting shown in the diagram (Plate IIb), the figure of Christ retains the original pose and, in general, the twelfth-century form and drapery arrangement.

Nevertheless, the hand of the restorer seems omnipresent, mostly because of the appalling nineteenth-century head, for which the restorer used the Greek Zeus of Olympia as a model.[1] In addition, a cutting-away from the underarm to the waist along the bared right side has reduced the silhouette of the figure. As a result, the proportions of the upper body gradually diminish above the waist, thus causing Christ to appear emaciated. In their visual impact, those two restorations modify the twelfth-century aesthetic more than the sum of all the other repairs to the figure.

An equally serious alteration obscured an important iconographical detail. In repairing Christ's severely damaged right side, the restorer apparently mistook the lozenge-shaped wound below his breast (caused by Longinus's spear) for an accidental gash or surface mutilation.[2] Obviously unaware of the significance of this detail, the restorer sealed the wound with mortar and

27

thus eliminated the raison d'être for Christ's bared right shoulder and side. Hardly visible today, the scar measures 7.25 by 2 cm. at its longest and widest points.

The relatively few areas where recutting has not affected the original surface include the right shoulder and arm, the splayed locks of hair on both shoulders, the left sleeve over the forearm, its jeweled border, and the left wrist. In the lower half of the figure, the drapery over the right knee, the jeweled border of the mantle directly below and in the center, and most of the ornamental band along the hem between Christ's feet also retain their twelfth-century surfaces. Elsewhere the pervasive recutting proved minor and caused little distortion to the drapery, with the following exceptions.

The most modified twelfth-century carving lies along the fracture that cuts through Christ's left leg, where various insets and attendant recutting deformed the contours but not the arrangement of the folds. Immediately to the left, recutting caused some asymmetry in the lowest V-shaped fold of the lap drapery. Repairs to the fracture also eliminated the outermost fold and the lowest foldback of the mantle by Christ's right leg, reduced the upper contours of the agitated swirl beside his left ankle, erased the lowest foldback of the adjacent hemline of the mantle, and created a slight distortion in the curve of the mandorla-like throne in that area. Equally heavy recutting of the mantle below Christ's outstretched arms reduced the folds to rudimentary ripples. Most of the rest of the recutting proved surprisingly light—so light that even in recut areas some good twelfth-century surfaces survive.

The survival of patches of original surfaces in recut areas, together with the unrecut portions listed above, provides important information. Without question, the unrecut right knee gives the original foremost projection of the lower half of the figure. Although mastic points up the damaged but generally unrecut ridges of the folds over the right thigh and between the knees, enough twelfth-century work survives in those bold and strongly modeled V-shaped folds to authenticate the arrangement. Despite the shaving and flattening of the ridges of the vertical folds of the underskirt, the plasticity of the modeling still strikes the viewer. A sense of substance and the depth of modeling, preoccupations of the original sculptor, survive in the pronounced undercutting along the hems and folded-back edges of the garments as well as in the lightly recut but still bulky engirdling drapery. Enough good surfaces remain to authenticate the shape and decoration of the mandorla-like throne.[3] The torus defining its outer edge shows considerable recutting and retains its fully rounded contours only on the lower left above the sarcophagus lid.

The prerestoration drawing of the west facade by the architects Cellérier and Legrand includes a small, schematic, but distorted representation of the figure of Christ (Fig. 3). The enlarged detail of the drawing (Fig. 4) clearly shows the bare right shoulder and arm, the drapery falling from the left shoulder, the draped and sleeved left arm, and the scrolls held in Christ's outstretched hands. The **V**-shaped folds between his knees are implied in the sketch, which also indicates the mandorla-like throne. The drawing, an approximate diagram of the figure we see today, confirms what careful examination has revealed: despite extensive recutting and except for the stylistically anomalous nineteenth-century head, the central figure of Christ retains the essence of the twelfth-century form.[4]

By enlarging the arms of the cross grotesquely and at the same time diminishing its upper portion, or head, absurdly, the Cellérier-Legrand drawing grossly distorted the proportions. Yet examination revealed the validity of what we see today. Even though almost the entire surface of the cross underwent a superficial recutting in the nineteenth century, traces of unrecut surfaces survive along its under edge and in the incised lines that emphasize its contours. Those twelfth-century surfaces verify the profile of the cross, the articulated knobs and flared ends, and the central disk at the junction of the arms and stem.[5] But as Guilhermy remarked, the gratuitous addition in 1840 of the letters INRI at the head of the cross placed an inappropriate monogram above the representation of the Christ of the Second Coming, or Last Judgment.[6]

The two scrolls extending from Christ's outstretched hands consist of twelfth-century stone of a piece with the upper tympanum lunette. Recut on the surface, the bands now bear inscriptions carved in 1840: on Christ's right, "Venite benedicti Patris mei" (Matthew 25:34); on his left, "Discedite a me maledicti" (Matthew 25:41).[7] Guilhermy wrote, "Les bras étendus tiennent deux légendes sur lesquelles on a gravé en 1840 à droite . . . [Matthew 25:34], à gauche . . . [Matthew 25:41]."[8] In that context the word *légendes* must refer to the scrolls and their generic function, not to the inscriptions. Thus we do not know from Guilhermy's comment whether traces of the twelfth-century inscriptions had survived to guide the restorer. The overall recutting of the surfaces of the banderoles was so light that in all probability the legends originally were painted rather than incised. Over the centuries, very little of a painted inscription could have survived unless it were renewed periodically. Yet, since the incised quotations from the Gospel of Matthew are traditional in the context of the Last Judgment, their validity seems probable.[9]

A few additional technical details observable in the figure of Christ deserve attention. The pressures that caused the upper tympanum fracture visible behind Christ's right arm seem to have been referred along the free-standing right arm to his wrist and the weakest, narrowest point where the thumb inset joins the arm. There the joint of the inset and the fracture become coextensive, the latter then continuing along the palm of the hand. The good twelfth-century surface behind the right arm indicates that the arm was always freestanding. Apparently worried by the fractures of the tympanum as well as the wrist fracture and adjacent thumb inset, the restorer backed the arm with reinforcing mortar, most of which has since fallen away. The *brettelé* marks, or striations, made by the nineteenth-century chisel are visible on the surface of the cross above the two-part inset that replaced both the right thumb and a small portion of the scroll. That portion of the scroll was set into the surface plane, but the excision of the original carving required by this repair seems surprisingly clumsy. The inset restoring the other thumb also has its upper joint in the surface behind it, although the structural necessity for such a procedure seems less than compelling.

In preparing to insert the new head, the restorer cut away most of the remnants of the original one, even though he consistently left stumps as backing for the insets replacing the Apostles' heads. The stone behind Christ's head is roughly hewn, and the surface is crosshatched with the tooth marks of the restorer's chisel. Across the neck and behind the fully undercut beard, the nineteenth-century head joins the twelfth-century body. However discordant the modern locks of hair framing the face may seem, the coiffure has confirmation in the surviving twists of twelfth-century hair that divide and splay across both shoulders. Here, as elsewhere, the nineteenth-century striations seem coarse and mechanical next to the twelfth-century convention for hair that they emulate.

The restoration has been unjustly condemned for the modeling of the torso, which articulates the bone structure of the collarbones, chest, and diaphragm, as well as for the scrawny, sinuous character of the right arm. Yet the patina of age on the unretouched surfaces of the arm identify it as twelfth-century carving; the exceptionally light recutting over the chest and frontal planes of the rib cage leaves no doubt that the twelfth-century sculptor gave form to the breast bone and ribs. The anatomical verisimilitude and the rounded form of the right arm reveal on a grand scale the same new interest in anatomy, sense of volume, and forward projection found in the sensitively modeled little bodies of the Resurrected Dead in the frieze along the lowest zone of the tympanum.

THE RESURRECTION FRIEZE

 Although some of the figures in the Resurrection frieze (nos. 11–19, Plates IIIa and IVa) have been heavily restored, careful examination revealed that much of the original sculpture has survived.[10] Even though some of the figures appear severely recut (nos. 11b, 12b, and 13a, Plate IIIb), and many losses of both original and nineteenth-century carving have occurred, with few exceptions either the original pose and gestures of the figure survive, or fragments— some still extant, others visible in earlier photographs—verify the poses and gestures as restored. In fact, the one figure that belongs almost entirely to the nineteenth century rests on a fragment of the original right buttock—a detail authenticating at least the seated pose (no. 17a, Plate IVb). In the same figure the bent left leg, a second fragment surviving from the twelfth century but now hidden by the nineteenth-century right arm and sarcophagus lid, confirms the restoration of this resurrected figure seated with her back to the central figure of Christ.

Although not one head has survived in the frieze, a number of torsos in proof condition deserve special note (see nos. 11c, 12a, and 12c, Plate IIIa–b, and nos. 18b and 19c, Plate IVa–b). The natural proportions, lively poses, and subtle modeling of those bodies show the artist's respect for and knowledge of human anatomy—a true reflection of the new attitudes that distinguish the nascent Gothic style. Several of the figures deserve further attention either because of their iconographical and stylistic importance or because they reveal techniques used by the restorer.

31

FIG. 10. Oblique view of Suger kneeling at the feet of Christ. Detail of frieze of the Resurrected Dead, lintel zone, left, no. 14

KNEELING FIGURE OF SUGER

Enough remnants of the original sculpture survive to reconstruct the silhouette of the twelfth-century figure identified as Suger (sarcophagus no. 14, Fig. 10 and Plate IIIa) and to verify his kneeling pose at the feet of Christ. A single nine-teenth-century inset encompasses the head, torso, arms and hands, and the right upper leg. The joining of the inset, sometimes lost under heavy white mortar and in roughened stone, becomes visible on the top of Suger's head despite an overlay of mastic (Fig. 10). The joint continues down the middle of the back of his head, shoulders, back, and buttocks, with the mastic overlay espe-cially heavy across his shoulders. The well-defined joint follows the contour of the right heel and calf, proceeds on a diagonal from his rump to the top of the knee, then turns upward at an acute angle to continue its course along the inside of his right thigh. The joint can then be traced with difficulty in the rough twelfth-century stone beneath the sleeves below the forearms, but it emerges clearly between the fingertips of the two hands. The twelfth-century remnants, although entirely recut, include the left thigh, right lower leg and foot, and a sliver of stone that forms the left buttock, back, shoulder, left side of the skull, and fingertips of the left hand. Those vestiges testify to the existence in the original iconographical program of this kneeling figure with hands in prayerful supplication. With the pose authenticated by the twelfth-century silhouette, the identification of the figure rests on the sole reference to the central tympanum in the writings of Abbot Suger. He mentioned an inscription, now lost, that originally appeared in *superliminari* (on the lintel):

> Receive, O stern Judge, the prayers of thy Suger;
> Grant that I be mercifully numbered among thy own sheep.[11]

Suger's sarcophagus appears so completely recut that no traces of the twelfth-century decoration survive, but behind the kneeling figure, the twelfth-century lid of his sarcophagus has retained its original patina. A comparison of Suger's smooth-shaven sarcophagus with the two on the far right (nos. 18 and 19, Fig. 11), indicates the type of ornamental detail erased by recutting. Beading surrounds every aperture in sarcophagus no. 18, and an incised line accents each tiny lancet piercing the surface of no. 19. Traces of decorative beading and outlining survive on three others (nos. 11, 12, and 15, Plates IIIa–b and IVa–b), but only the two on the far right retain pristine twelfth-century surfaces. Presumably similar details embellished the architectural elements of the other four clean-shaven sarcophagi.

FIGURE OF A BISHOP OR KING

This figure (sarcophagus no. 16a, Plate IVa) raises interesting iconographical questions that cannot be answered with certainty but which seem worth considering. The diagram shows insets, recutting, and a new head crowned with a poor approximation of a twelfth-century bishop's or abbot's miter. Although the height of the headgear as restored seems correct for a miter, it also vaguely

33

FIG. 11.   Frieze of the
Resurrected Dead.
Detail of lintel zone, right,
nos. 18a–b and 19a–b

suggests the profile of a crown. The headdress also lacks the lateral peaks
and the lappets that characterized twelfth-century miters, although the recutting and mastic overlay on the shoulder could have eliminated all traces of
the lappets. The nineteenth-century hand, now lost, was raised, but not in the
gesture of blessing appropriate to a bishop. Earlier photographs show the
hand open, palm facing out, in a gesture of adulation or acclaim now impossible to verify. Neither the gesture nor the attribute held in the left hand
resolves the identity of the figure. The shape of the attribute, a small round
object capped with a worn and poorly articulated node, suggests either an orb
or a pomegranate. The orb, a royal symbol, should be carried with the emblem
upright, but here the small protuberance tilts forward. Therefore it is probably
a pomegranate, an attribute equally appropriate for a resurrected king or
bishop in expectation of immortality.[12]

MUTILATED FIGURE

The loss of a portion of the nineteenth-century inset that replaced the head,
arms, and chest of this figure (sarcophagus no. 18a, Fig. 11 and Plate IVb)
demonstrates to perfection some of the techniques employed by the restorer.
The triangular wedge that has fallen away reveals not only the surface of the old
stone prepared to receive the inset, but also the upper portion of the pinning
dowel still set into a hole that formed a pocket for the mortar (Fig. 11). The area,

a gaping inverted **V**, shows the surface of the twelfth-century stone smoothed and cut away on an inclined, stepped-back plane nearly to the level of the navel. The lost inset originally replaced the head, shoulders, upper torso, and all but the left elbow of the folded arms. Certainly too large in relation to the scale of the figure, the metal dowel, which had expanded and contracted with seasonal temperature changes, finally caused the loss of a portion of the restoration. Although the legs, hips, and lower abdomen consist of good unre-cut twelfth-century carving, not enough survives to reconstruct the original pose. The remnant of the left elbow, which required a bent left arm, makes the arrangement plausible, if not certain.

CONTORTED FIGURE

The adjacent figure in the same sarcophagus (sarcophagus no. 18b, Fig. 11 and Plate IVb) reveals an earlier stage in the degenerative process, caused by the expansion and contraction of the pinning dowel. The splintering of the stone has already resulted in the loss of a wedge of old stone over the right rib cage (Fig. 11). A diagonal fracture runs from the upper right corner of the scar and continues through the joint of the nineteenth-century head at the base of the neck, across the chin, mouth, and into the left cheek, where it ends at the transverse fracture that bisects the restored head. Hairline cracks, portending the loss of another portion of the figure, define another rectangular section of old stone on the right side of the chest.

Because the figure provides one of the best-preserved examples of the lively twelfth-century figurate style and of the formal skill of the sculptor of the Resurrection frieze, its impending disintegration seems particularly unfortunate. The marvelously contorted but entirely plausible arrangement of the arms, the diagonal thrust of the lightly modeled torso, the bent right leg tensed to assist the upward impulse implicit in the right hand, not only reflect the physical effort necessary to raise the sarcophagus lid and emerge from the grave, but also reveal the artist's concern for anatomical reality, as well as his skill in rendering it.

HAIR-PULLING FIGURE

35

In this figure (sarcophagus no. 19a, Fig. 11 and Plate IVb) another twelfth-century pose has survived, spared by both the iconoclasts and the restorer, who replaced only the head and lightly recut the left hand (Fig. 11). The new head joins the body at the base of the throat; the lateral lines of joining conform to the contours of the head. The fists grabbing the locks of hair proved original— a lively conceit with a counterpart in gesture at the opposite end of the Resurrection frieze.

COQUETTISH WOMAN ADJUSTING HER COIFFURE

Except for her head, left forearm, and hand, the figure of the woman (sarcophagus no. 11b, Plate IIIb) appears well preserved. Her acutely bent left elbow survives from the original carving and, as the factor determining the position of the new left forearm, authenticates her natural and feminine gesture. The pose suggests that at the moment of resurrection, the woman's first thought was for her appearance. Nearly freestanding, her delicately modeled body, naturally proportioned and anatomically correct, testifies to the artist's respect for the integrity of the human figure.

As a whole, differentiated not only by pose but also by sex, and even reflecting psychological differences, the figures of the frieze of the Resurrected Dead express the artist's concern for and awareness of traits that would distinguish individual types. The eye traveling across the lintel zone finds the coquette, the glutton, the demure, the pious, the vigorous, the lowly, and the mighty all represented and characterized in this animated row, awaiting judgment.

The artist responsible for the Resurrection frieze also carved other sections of the portal. We will gradually discover sculpture attributable to his hand in the lunette of the tympanum, in the figures on axis in the four archivolts, in the scenes of the Blessed and Damned on the innermost archivolt, and on the two jambs of the doorway. We have noted that in the Resurrection frieze he carved figures of natural but solid proportions that were anatomically correct, delicately modeled, and carefully differentiated. His treatment of draperies in the clothed figures and individualistic handling of drapery conventions set him apart from the two other masters whose work can be identified in the central portal. We will call this artist the Master of the Tympanum Angels, because those four figures represent his crowning achievement. The second master, styled the Master of the Apostles, carved the row of figures above the Resurrection

36

FIG. 12. Nineteenth-century head, view from left. Detail of Apostle no. 33, tympanum, far right

frieze, but not the central figure of Christ. As we survey the sculptural ensemble and perceive the stylistic proclivities and preferences embodied in the work of each master, evidence will accumulate to attribute the figure of Christ to a third artist, the Master of the Elders (or patriarchs), who was responsible for those twenty-four figures in the three outer archivolts.

THE APOSTLES, VIRGIN, AND FLANKING ANGELS

None of the figures of the Apostles in the middle zone of the tympanum (nos. 21–26, 28–33, Plates IIIb and IVb) escaped damage or the heavy hand of the restorer. Nevertheless, despite the fact that all heads belong to the nineteenth-century restoration, and a scattering of insets and recutting repair the random damage to the drapery, hands, and feet, much survives to reveal the richness and forceful character of those twelfth-century figures and the hand of the master who carved them. The restoration did not diminish their substantial, solid forms, nor did it alter their varied but restrained poses and gestures—all part of a well-ordered, rhythmic composition that avoided the tedium of a frieze of uniform figures.

Unfortunately the nineteenth-century heads have a shocking visual impact, even though some of the features and arrangements of hair and beard emulate characteristics of one of the mutilated twelfth-century heads from Saint-Denis now in the Louvre.[13] The similarities between the nineteenth-century head of Apostle no. 33 and the Louvre head (cat. no. 53) suggest that the

37

FIG. 13a. Twelfth-century head from Saint-Denis. Paris, Musée du Louvre, cat. no. 53. The head originally belonged to patriarch N, second archivolt, right

FIG. 13b. Plaster cast of Louvre head (cat. no. 53) juxtaposed to the nineteenth-century head in situ of patriarch N

FIG. 14. Twelfth-century heads from Saint-Denis originally belonging to Apostles nos. 21 and 22, tympanum, left. Paris, Musée du Louvre, cat. no. 54

restorer had either that twelfth-century head or a similar one before him as a model (Figs. 12 and 13a). In the restored head, the hair convention, the arrangement of the beard, the broad forehead, spreading nose, wide philtrum, full lips, as well as the wide-set eyes and protruding eyeballs rimmed with wide bands representing the eyelids all seem an inept and bland parody of those same characteristics in the Louvre head.

Although the actual dimensions of the twelfth-century head proved congruent not with the Apostles' heads, but with the archivolt figures,[14] two smaller attached heads (Louvre cat. no. 54, Fig. 14) have dimensions compatible with the Apostles' measurements and consonant with the figures of Apostles nos. 21 and 22 on the far left (Plate IIIa). In addition to their correct proportions, the angle and length of the diagonal break or cut across the necks of the Louvre pair and the combined width of their heads (measured on a horizontal line drawn from the upper edge of the break across under the beards) correspond exactly to equivalent measurements taken along a horizontal line below the beards joining the modern heads of the two Apostles. The greatest

39

depth of the Louvre heads, measured along the break, falls within the tolerance of the greatest forward projection of the twelfth-century bodies along the diagonal line that joined the new heads.[15] In those telling measurements, which indicate a perfect match of the twelfth-century heads with the original bodies, we must note a single discrepancy. The restored heads face away from each other, whereas the Louvre heads are parallel and face frontally. Yet the latter agree perfectly with the frontal poses of the shoulders and torsos of the two Apostles, and the placement of the left head sightly forward of the right one also suits the relationship of the two bodies.

A portion of the original head of Apostle no. 33, on the far right, survives in situ (Plate IVb). That generous remnant provides an additional control in evaluating the proportions and positions of the nineteenth-century heads, as well as their projection from the background plane. The twelfth-century remnant to which the nineteenth-century restoration of the head of Apostle no. 33 is attached includes the hair framing the right side of his face. The line of joining coincides with the hairline along his cheek, but at the temple the joint enters the hair. Circling over the top of his head, the mortar joint moves forward to descend on the viewer's right, so that the twelfth-century fragment includes the entire back of the turned head and some of the hair at the back of the neck. The fully rounded form of the twelfth-century remnant does not stand free but nestles in the crook of the angel's wing stretching above and behind the Apostle. The fragment verifies the turn of the head, which also agrees with the alignment of the shoulders. Then, too, since the vestige includes the top of the head, it also preserved the head-to-body proportions of the seated figure, and, by extension, verifies the dimensions of the other heads as restored. With the exception noted in Apostles nos. 21 and 22, the rest of the Apostle heads all follow the dictates of the twelfth-century torsos and align either with the shoulders of the figure or, in the case of Apostle no. 32, with the focus of his attention. In that row of seated figures, the turn of the heads and bodies makes a significant contribution to the overall composition.

The formal organization of the Apostle frieze, with its planned movement and visual balance, emerges as an important characteristic of the sculptural ensemble—one that distinguishes it from its Romanesque predecessors. Depicted in apostolic dialogue, or *in disputatione,* those conversing Apostles carry on a tradition that goes back to Late Antiquity and signifies the essential function of Christ's disciples as teachers of men. Medieval teaching took the form of *disputatio,* a discussion or debate about what is truth and what is falsehood.[16] The six Apostles on the left form two distinct groups of three figures. Within each group the figures relate to each other not only through their poses and gestures, but also in the arrangement of the folds of their draperies. Even the ornamental borders of their garments seem to band them together. The inside of the back hems functions similarly, enclosing three pairs of feet in each group, whereas the opposed swirls of the mantles and tunics of Apostles nos. 22 and 23 punctuate the grouping as emphatically as their figures turned in opposite directions (Plate IIIa). The arrangement of the Apostles on the right has even greater sophistication. The six break down into pairs that are either linked by gesture or represented *in disputatione* (Plate IVa). In counterpoint to the pairing, the artist has created two groups of three. That second division actually interrupts the conversation of the middle pair. Yet the identical unifying elements or devices used to link the trios on the left side of the tympanum create the grouping into threes on the right.

The authenticity of the gestures, as important to the iconography as to the composition, has been questioned in the past. Von Borries suggested that the Apostles originally held books and scrolls, their customary attributes, and that the Virgin (no. 27, Plate IIIb) should have been restored with one hand resting on her breast, the other holding a book. Dismissing her gesture as "groteske," he interpreted the hand that holds the veil to her face not as the traditional gesture of mourning, but simply as the Virgin touching her veil to her nose.[17] In fact, the Virgin's elongated, softly rounded hands, her veil, and the crumpled, or goffered, inner sleeves delicately ornamented at the cuffs all consist of original unrecut stone (Fig. 15a). Touched only by age and weather, they provide unspoiled examples of the deft and sensitive twelfth-century carving, as does the elegant, ornamental border along the hem of her gown. The beading still visible along the seam on the toes of her pointed slippers adds a felicitous, realistic touch (Fig. 15b).

Guilhermy told an amusing anecdote with reference to the original restoration of the figure of the Virgin. Soon after the scaffolding was removed, an astute observer commented on the fact that there were thirteen Apostles at Saint-Denis, all of them with beards and mustaches. The "thirteenth Apostle" was, of course, the Virgin seated on Christ's right. At Didron's insistence,

FIG. 15a. Twelfth-century hands and nineteenth-century head of Virgin, no. 27, seated at Christ's right, tympanum, left

FIG. 15b. Ornament along the hem of the tunic and the slippered feet of Virgin, no. 27

Guilhermy wrote, "Quelques coups de ciseau lui ont donné, tant bien que mal, une expression plus féminine."[18] "A few cuts of the chisel" somewhat underestimates the measures needed to rectify the initial error and achieve a "more feminine expression." Two nineteenth-century joints, one directly under the Virgin's chin and another nearer the base of her neck, indicate that a second head was carved and most of the first one removed to make way for it (Fig. 15a).

The examination of the sculpture also authenticated the beautifully preserved hands of Apostles nos. 21 and 30 (Fig. 9 and Plate IIIa). Their fully undercut hands, like those of the Virgin, seem remarkable for their softly rounded forms, which contrast so blatantly with the clumsy nineteenth-century replacements. Note especially the restored hands of Apostles nos. 25 and 28 (Plates IIIb and IVb). The equally well-preserved right hand of Apostle no. 32 represents a different hand type (Plate IVb). Distinguished by the delicate articulation of the bone structure, this elongated and anatomically explicit hand proves more characteristic of the hands of the archivolt figures than of the Apostles (patriarchs A, G, Q, and R, Plates VI–VIII). This juxtaposition of distinct and unrelated styles emerges as one of the prevailing characteristics of the sculpture of the portal. The authentication of two or more distinct stylistic elements in the work of one artist at first surprises, but, in the final analysis, increases our understanding of the interaction of ideas in the exciting artistic environment which Suger's building campaigns encouraged.

The diagrams of the Apostle zone identify not only those surprisingly well-preserved hands, but also indicate all the minor repairs to the other hands

(Plates IIIb and IVb). Without exception, the restorations followed the requirements of the surviving portion of the forearms, wrists, and hands. Even the
poorly executed inset replacing both hands of Apostle no. 25 has authentication
in the twelfth-century cuffs still intact and visible behind the new hands. The
stumps indicate that the original hands were freestanding, upraised, and close
together. The prayerful attitude of the new hands therefore seems entirely
probable. The upraised remnant of the forearm of Apostle no. 28, on Christ's
left, also determined the placement of the new left hand, if not the curling
fingertips. That position, the hand touching the chin, is one of many variants on
the gesture of mourning. Since the Apostle is turning toward Christ and is not
depicted *in disputatione* with his neighbor, the gesture seems quite appropriate
and raises the question whether originally the figure on Christ's left was that of
the beardless John. Many representations of the Deisis show John making the
same gesture as restored here.[19] Possibly a Deisis was originally intended in conjunction with the Last Judgment instead of the Crucifixion, but evidence does
not suffice to establish definitively that such a juxtaposition was an iconographical innovation originating at Saint-Denis.[20]

The hands of the angel with the flaming sword at the right end of the row
of Apostles (no. 34, Plate IVb) follow the arrangement proposed by the original
wrists and heel of the right hand. Assuming that both angels in the Apostle zone
were those of the Second Coming sent forth "with a trumpet, and a great
voice" to gather the elect (Matthew 24:31), von Borries dismissed the flaming
sword as a nineteenth-century invention and proposed a trumpet as the original attribute.[21] Yet the unrecut surface of the angel's chest indicates that the
original attribute was not held near his lips in a manner paralleling the trumpeting angel at the left end of the Apostle frieze (Plate IIIb). Then, too, the
angel's movement toward the closed door below that represents the gate of
Paradise clearly associates him with the gate and with the figure of the Foolish
Virgin kneeling before the barred door—a relationship that gives credence to
the sword as his attribute. Apparently the shut door referred to Matthew
25:10–12 and the parable of the ten virgins in which the symbolic door to
Paradise was closed to exclude forever the five Foolish Virgins who symbolized
the Damned. But the angel's attribute also refers to the cherubim with the
flaming sword placed at the Gate to Paradise after the expulsion: "And he
[the Lord] cast out Adam; and placed before the paradise of pleasure

43

Cherubims, and a flaming sword . . . to keep the way to the tree of life" (Genesis 3:24). The outsized bolt quite literally barring the door emphasizes New Testament imagery of the parable, just as the flaming sword attaches Old Testament imagery to the angel guarding the gate.

Although controversy also surrounds the restoration of the Apostles' feet, the diagrams indicate that all of the repairs, for the most part minor, followed the requirements of the twelfth-century sculpture. Von Borries questioned the arrangement of the inset replacing the right leg and foot of Apostle no. 23 (Plate IIIb).[22] Even though extremely inept and stylistically incongruous, the restoration perpetuated the original pose—the only possible arrangement that accords with existing circumstances. First and foremost, the area around the lower leg and foot appears unrecut. In addition, the crossed leg of the inset follows the dictates of the elevated right thigh and of the fragment of the original hand resting on the raised knee. Finally, the crowding of the feet of the first three Apostles allows no room on the footrest for another foot.

The arrangement of Apostles nos. 21 and 22 (Plate IIIa) represents an original and amusing solution to the problem of limited space. A similar overcrowding occurs on the far right, and in both instances the artist eschewed the Romanesque solution which, when space was limited, required only the correct count of heads. Striving for greater naturalism, the Saint-Denis artist took pains to represent the correct number of feet as well, and at least to suggest twelve bodies by actually seating Apostle no. 21 on the lap of no. 22, whose right foot pokes out from beneath the back hem of the Apostle on his lap. Even the small wedge of skirt drapery above his crowded left foot has a different ornamental border—another cryptic indication of his presence. The novel arrangement has a counterpart in the feet of Apostles nos. 25 and 26 (Plate IIIa); the latter has firmly planted his right foot on the instep of his neighbor.[23] Space was limited, and as the diagram shows, in both instances either the original feet or adequate remnants survive to verify the poses and the twelfth-century conceits.

In contrast to those inventive but naive arrangements, which nevertheless reflect the artist's attitude of respect for the integrity of the human form, the pose of Apostle no. 31 looks back toward the more stylized Romanesque manipulation of the human body (Plate IVa). Although notable for their delicate articulation, his feet are presented in a highly stylized, unnatural pose evoking the Romanesque convention of crossed legs with feet confronted and *sur les pointes*. Yet like the feet of Apostle no. 33 (Fig. 16c), which also deserve mention for their elegant pose and beautiful modeling, the feet of no. 31 reflect the same careful observation of natural forms that characterizes the carving of the right hand of Apostle no. 32, the third member of the group.

The diagrams show at a glance that a great deal of extremely fine drapery has survived in those mid-tympanum figures. Untouched areas predominate and provide excellent examples of the way in which folds were manipulated to define the forms beneath. The figures in the frieze unite a sense of volume and substance with restrained gestures. Rich ornamentation and a subtle interplay of curves enliven every figure (especially no. 28, Figs. 16a–b and Plate IVa). The striving for accuracy in such details as the well-preserved border ornament contrasts with the more stylized but always vigorous draperies. The recutting never altered the basic arrangement of the Apostles' drapery, although in a few instances the restorer cut back the surfaces enough to blur or diminish the clarity of the folds (see recut areas as diagrammed: Apostles nos. 21, 23, 24, 28, 31, and 33, and angels nos. 20 and 34, Plates IIIb and IVb).[24]

Even in the heavily recut figures, much survives that preserves the work of the twelfth-century carver. In the figure of the trumpeting angel (no. 20, Plate IIIb), the flaring folds that sweep from hip to hem in a gravity-defying curve give authority to the angel who stands no higher than the seated figures. At the opposite end of the tympanum, the powerful impression created by the angel's figure accrues from its striking formal attributes (no. 34, Plate IV). The strong diagonals of the skirt drapery and hemline emphasize the thrust of weight from the right to the left leg. Together with the counter-diagonals of the left wing and sword, they underscore the angel's movement toward the barred Gate to Paradise and forcefully punctuate the right end of the frieze. The broadly conceived folds that encircle his right thigh—a convention subject to infinite variations, which occurs throughout the portal—in this figure firmly establish the anatomy of the leg beneath.

The artist demonstrated his skillful close observation of natural forms through a number of delightful devices, for instance the ripples of the borders of the garments as they break over the instep (Apostle no. 28, Fig. 16b). The arrangement subtly communicates not only the weight of the embroidered

45

FIG. 16a.   Left sleeve of Apostle no. 28, tympanum, right

FIG. 16b.   Drapery over legs of Apostle no. 28

FIG. 16c.   Drapery over legs of Apostle no. 32, tympanum, right

and jewel-encrusted borders, but also the volume of the foot beneath (see also angel no. 20, Apostles nos. 21 and 25, and the Virgin, no. 27). The deeply modeled opulent folds and thick edges of the tunics and mantles, with their folded-back hems, give texture as well as weight to the fabrics (especially in the robes of angel no. 20, Apostles nos. 24 and 28, and the Virgin, no. 27). In all the figures, the artist manipulated stylized drapery conventions to reveal their solid forms. Stylized folds typical of the Languedoc—a convention distinguished by the narrow, articulated ridge that accents the crease of each fold—curve across the thighs (especially Apostles nos. 29, 30, and 33, Fig. 16c) or define the arm (Apostle no. 28, Fig. 16a). Folds with creases that cut into the flesh curve across the arms (angel no. 20 and Apostles nos. 23, 24, and 28). Concentric U-shaped folds clamp tightly around upper and lower legs (the Virgin, no. 27, and Apostles nos. 28, 29, 32, and 33), and encircling folds occasionally accent the bend of a knee (Apostles nos. 29, 30, and 33, Fig. 16c). The artist used those drapery conventions with restraint on the left side of the tympanum, but on the right he created richer, more turbulent patterns. Yet he also achieved a visual balance by endowing the figures on the left with a greater salience from the surface plane.

The Virgin (no. 27, Plate IIIa) and Apostle no. 28 (Plate IVa), at Christ's right and left, epitomize his contrasting treatment of the two groups. Presented in a three-quarter view so that her right shoulder overlaps that of her neighbor, the Virgin exists in three-dimensional space and has plausibility as a seated figure. Her person, gestures, and drapery consist of a series of overlapping forms enriched by the interplay of curves. The somewhat clumsy convention suggesting the effect of the seat of the bench on the heavy fabric of the skirt of her tunic adds to the impression of depth and projection by means of bold modeling and the flaring, undercut convolution of the hem. Encrusted with embroidery and jewels, the hem has a much less active line than that of Apostle no. 28 (Figs. 15b and 16b). The sense of projection of his broader, heavier figure seems somewhat diminished by the liveliness of the surface patterns of the drapery. Broadly conceived parallel folds curve across his chest, and folds accented with an incised line near the ridges define the contours of his left arm. Those highly stylized conventions contrast with the deep foldback of the mantle that responds realistically to the form of the left knee (Fig. 16a). The strongly modeled folds flanking his legs—a repetition of verticals located below the slashing diagonal of his richly ornamented mantle (Fig. 16b)—provide a needed variant on the constant circular motion of the folds on the upper body, of those that loop across his knees and shanks, and of the U-shaped drapery that defines his lap. The vigorous handling of each drapery convention gives strength and importance to a figure otherwise dwarfed by the overpowering central figure of Christ. On the other side of the throne, the authority given to the figure of the Virgin by means of her pose, the interplay of broadly conceived curves, the heavy fabrics of her garments, and the solidity of her projecting form provides the requisite visual balance to Apostle no. 28.

The entire frieze of seated figures, forcefully presented but balanced and beautifully organized, reveals the Apostle Master's highly developed formal sophistication, his interest in natural forms and in textures, and his delight in varied and sumptuous detail. Although he used Romanesque drapery conventions, he also manipulated them to emphasize the solid volumes beneath. The interesting and varied figures, in which the artist juxtaposed stylizations with naturalistic effects, embody the tensions of opposing ideas. As a result, such details as the handling of a sleeve, the drapery of a mantle, or the folds defining a leg (Figs. 15a and 16a–c) often give greater pleasure than the figure as a whole. This fascinating and surprisingly well-preserved portion of the sculpture of the central portal deserved a better fate than marriage with the visually devitalizing nineteenth-century heads.

THE LUNETTE WITH TYMPANUM ANGELS

As a group, the four angels of the upper tympanum zone (nos. II–V, Plate IIc–d) suffered less in the hands of the restorer than the sculpture of the lower zones. These fluent and harmonious figures that retain so much of the twelfth-century aesthetic seem particularly incompatible with the monotonous facial style of the nineteenth-century heads. As the diagramming shows, the insets replacing three of the heads join the twelfth-century torsos approximately along the collar lines (angels nos. II–IV). The repair of the head of angel no. V on the far right, the best preserved of the four, involved an inset replacing only the face. Most of the original head survives as an excellent example of a highly stylized twelfth-century coiffure with finely drawn, striated hair. This coiffure probably provided the model for the restored locks of the companion figure at the far left (angel no. II). But in emulating the arrangement, the nineteenth-century sculptor produced harsh caricatures of the delicately carved, separated locks which frame the forehead of angel no. V.

Two of the restored heads seem to compromise the twelfth-century design in still another respect. The positions of the new heads of the two angels flanking the cross (angels nos. III and IV) fail to comply with surviving vestiges of the original hair spreading across their shoulders. Raised too high, the heads interrupt the continuous line proposed by the twelfth-century remnants.

The same two central angels carry objects of Christ's Passion—all nineteenth-century insets—and no fragments of the original objects have survived to authenticate the restorations. Yet the position of the angels' hands indicates that originally three attributes existed, two held by no. III and one by no. IV. Hovering on Christ's left, angel no. IV holds the least controversial attribute, the Crown of Thorns. His twelfth-century arms frame a space quite appropriate for such a circular object, yet unquestionably the twelfth-century crown would have been less coarse and prominent.

49

Separated, cupped hands covered by a single veil indicate that angel no. III originally presented two objects. Most of the nineteenth-century restoration in his right hand has fallen away; only the stone stumps of two square nineteenth-century nails remain to the left of a round brass dowel that projects from the center of the broken inset. At the right of the brass dowel, visible from above and flush with the cupped hand, the square-cornered outline of the joint of the inset indicates the dimensions of a lost portion of the nineteenth-century replacement. The original size and shape of the repair provide strong evidence that the restoration, if not the original representation, included four nails carved of stone.[25] The fragments certify that the restorer intended to represent the four that attached Christ to the cross, but the dowel of brass presents a puzzle for two reasons. At 0.75 cm. in diameter, it is much larger than all nineteenth-century pinning dowels now visible. In addition, those dowels are made of iron. This anomalous brass dowel raises an unanswerable question: was the original attribute in this angel's right hand a single nail—a reference to the one nail listed at Saint-Denis among the treasured relics of the Passion, along with thorns from the Crown of Thorns?[26]

The other attribute, a freestanding block of nineteenth-century stone in the angel's left hand, presents an even greater puzzle. It has an irregular, roughened upper surface with incisions or striations on both of the faces visible from below. Apparently intended to represent a broken piece of wood symbolizing a portion of the True Cross, the attribute seems questionable because of its redundancy, inasmuch as the two outer angels, nos. II and V, are supporting the arms of the cross that backs the central figure of Christ.[27] Unfortunately, no fragments of the original attribute have survived to provide clues justifying any other proposal concerning the nature or iconography of the twelfth-century object.[28]

On the left side of the tympanum, both wings of angel no. II and the right wing of no. III date from the restoration. The sharp contours and the lack of delicacy in the surface articulation seem at complete stylistic variance with the twelfth-century wings. Close examination indicated that in their placement, the restorations perpetuated the original arrangement. On the far left and directly to the left of the fissure in the upper tympanum stone, the twelfth-century tip of the right wing of angel no. II survives against the foliate molding. That small fragment authenticates both the size and the position of the replacement. Behind the left wing, the surface plane shows extensive gouging and roughness caused by the removal of the original wing. As well as verifying the placement of the modern wing, the gouging also revealed a metal dowel inserted from the inside to clamp one of the interior reinforcing slabs attached to the tympanum.[29] Bolts secure the new wings to the upper tympanum stone, and mortar hides the screw heads in the surface of the wings.

On the opposite side of the tympanum, both wings of angel no. V survive from the twelfth century. Covered with finely drawn overlapping feathers, their surfaces completely escaped recutting. Yet the fracture that crosses the angel's right wing apparently threatened its survival. To the right of the fracture the restorer therefore sliced off and removed the front face of the entire shoulder of the wing, then shaved back the remnant to the level of the background plane and reset the shoulder in white cement built up from the surface plane. In so doing, he closed the gap caused by the tympanum fracture so that the reset section of the wing now interrupts its course. Similar cement backing also reinforces the same angel's left wing as well as the original left wing of angel no. III. Although each of the other three extant twelfth-century wings in the upper tympanum group has a nineteenth-century patch (see angels nos. III and IV), the deft and delicate modeling of the original surface feathers shows no recutting.

The placement of all those beautiful wings deserves particular attention, since it reflects new ideas that distinguish the sculpture at Saint-Denis from that of earlier portals. The artist of the lunette did not fully accept the restrictions of the frame. The wings of all four angels violate its confines; they spread across the foliate molding that encloses the tympanum (as do those of the two angels at either end of the Apostle frieze). Nor did the artist allow the crowding typical of many Romanesque Last Judgment scenes, with the attendant distortions caused by confining human and animal forms within the strictures of an allotted space or of an ornamental design. Although the horizontal poses of the angels as well as their placement accommodate to the shallow curve of the lunette-shaped stone, the sculptor nonetheless created figures with credible proportions. He adapted them to the spatial limitations by overlapping the figures— a treatment that gives them additional reality in terms of three-dimensional space. The same balance, order, and clearly defined spatial relationships that characterize the lower zones also prevail in the upper lunette.

The restorer may have thought to improve on the twelfth-century sculptor's illusion of space by cutting back the surface plane above the figures of the

51

angels. That change, an alteration rather than a repair, increased the visual impression of the forward projection of the figures. The recutting begins at the left between the wings of angel no. II, where it also flattens the torus. Continuing to the right, recutting increasingly affects the surface plane above the figure of angel no. III. The areas to the left and right of the stem of the cross, however, appear unrecut and provide a control establishing both the original surface level of the background and also the profile of the roll molding. The severe recutting resumes between the wings of the angel to the right of the cross (angel no. IV), where it reduces the width of the foliate band as much as 4 cm. and again flattens the torus. The drastic cutting-back continues into and terminates in the area between the wings of the angel on the far right. Although light recutting occurs along the upper surface of that angel's body and over both feet, the adjacent surface plane and the foliate molding show absolutely none. Higher up, the cutting-back of the surface plane extended behind the wings, which magnifies the viewer's sense both of depth and of forward projection. On the right, where the shaving-back and distortion are greatest, recutting actually altered the curve of the arc of the lunette, but the wings and surrounding foliage survive in excellent condition—evidence that the change in the level of the surface plane could not have represented a needed repair.

The recutting becomes explicable only as an effort to impose the restorer's aesthetic preference on the twelfth-century artist's work. The initials MB in Roman lettering were cut into the surface plane to the left of the cross. An identical monogram recurs on the cut-back surface above the southeastern capital of the hemicycle of the crypt. Perhaps proud of his contribution, the restorer who tampered with the surface plane did not wish to remain entirely anonymous.[30]

Damage to the sculpture, not an aesthetic preference, dictated the recutting of the background to the right of the veiled hands of angel no. III and to the left of no. IV. The recutting eliminated portions of the veil fluttering from the angels' hands across the surface plane. The loop of the scarf that encircles the right arm of the latter angel shows the loss of at least one outer fold. For the most part, however, the recutting of the drapery of all four angels proved surprisingly light, so light that it modified but did not eliminate all traces of surface damage. The heaviest recutting occurred on the left hand and along the scarf covering the left wrist of angel no. II, on the right and left shoulders respectively of angels nos. III and IV, and on the left hand of the angel on the far right. Yet those skinned areas still have surface scars and abrasions, and even the teardrop folds, a significant stylistic hallmark of the Master of the Tympanum Angels, survived the light recutting.

As well as the teardrop fold, the four angels share a number of conventions that distinguish the Angel Master's hand. In forming that stylized teardrop, he characteristically added two short, parallel curving lines on the ridge just beyond the depression. They enclose the cavity in the same way that quotation marks set off spoken words in a sentence. When occurring in the scarves and sashes, those deep, narrow creases that terminate in a teardrop seem designed to enliven and vary the lines of parallel folds as the drapery curves around the upper bodies and loops over the arms. The fluid, linear patterns created by the multifolds of the scarves help to define anatomies and elaborate gesture. The draperies of the scarves reveal the artist's fascination and obvious delight in the interplay of curves. The various conventions that define the legs and thighs show the same preoccupation with curving lines repeated in a series. Overlapping folds encircle the smooth-ridged thighs and knees. (See especially angels nos. II and V.) The sculptor frequently enriched the clapboardlike drapery framing the legs with ridges that accent the edge of each fold in a manner considered typical of Romanesque sculpture in the Languedoc. Tubular hook folds, defined by creases that cut into the flesh of the leg, curve around the thighs and shins and advance the sense of volume and form beneath the drapery. One of the tubular folds in the perfectly preserved leg drapery of angel no. V pinpoints the knee by completely encircling it (compare also the left elbow of angel no. IV), and the cascade of drapery falling from the left hip flows into an unusual sickle-shaped hook that loops around the bend of the knee. Those encircling folds accenting the joints come from the vast storehouse of Romanesque drapery conventions from which this artist drew freely. Always partial to the curving line, the sculptor preferred the U-shaped to the V-shaped fold; although occasionally the lowest fold in one of the concentric series sharpens and approaches an angled V, as, for instance, in the drapery below the right hand of angel no. V.

This versatile master also preferred active silhouettes for the hemlines of the garments, scarves, veils, and sashes. But instead of splaying or spreading apart, the inner edges of his symmetrical underfolds meet in the center. That preference contrasts with the splayed inner edges of the foldbacks along the hem of the seated Christ of the tympanum, as well as the typical handling of that detail in the drapery of the patriarchs (see figures N and O, Plate VIIIa). The best examples of the Angel Master's treatment occur in the series of overlapping pleats in the veils covering the hands of angels nos. III and IV, and in the trailing scarves of angels II and V. Those convoluted edges, thick, but softly rounded, also typify the texture and weight that the master gave to fabrics.

The varied gestures of the angels animate the essentially symmetrical arrangement of the carefully composed group. The lower legs and feet of the central angels lie behind the heads and shoulders of the outer two. Thus, by overlapping the figures the artist was able to preserve their normal proportions and create significant empty, undecorated spaces on either side of Christ's head. The deliberate use of voids focused attention on the central theme. Such didactic clarity signals a concept of design quite unlike the familiar overall patterns of Romanesque compositions, which give the impression of a horror vacui.

Marked by their unity in style and composition, the four tympanum angels have strong stylistic affinities with the best preserved figures in the inner archivolt and with the jamb figures of the Wise and Foolish Virgins. The scenes of the first, or inner archivolt depict the fulfillment of Christ's judgments as related in the gospel of Matthew.

CHAPTER 4

THE JUDGMENT AND TRINITY
OF THE CENTER ARCHIVOLTS

THE JUDGING CHRIST

On the keystone, the focal point of the inner archivolt, the bust of Christ (no. X, Fig. 17 and Plate Va) represents the "Son of man coming in clouds of heaven with much power and great majesty" (Matthew 24:30). The restoration provided the usual bland and prominent nineteenth-century head. Projecting 3.5 cm. at its greatest salience from the surface of the keystone, a fragment of the original head provides the complete silhouette that verifies the head-to-body proportions of the replacement. As the diagram indicates, nineteenth-century *couvres-joints* and mortar repaired the badly eroded masonry joints of the keystone. Reflecting the wide separation of the left joint, the misalignment of the voussoirs has so distorted the circular nimbus that it now has an oval shape. On both sides of that joint, very light recutting skinned the surfaces of Christ's hair and the *galon,* the broad ornamental band at the neck of his tunic.

The insets replacing the hands have their joints in the surface plane, and neither hand as restored is authenticated by twelfth-century vestiges. Yet the blessing gesture of Christ's right hand seems correct and compatible with the text of Matthew 25:34: "Come, ye blessed of my Father, possess you the kingdom prepared for you from the foundation of the world." The left hand, open, with palm facing out, would be equally appropriate for the rejection of the lost soul on his left: "Depart from me, you cursed, into everlasting fire which was prepared for the devil and his angels" (Matthew 25:41). Then, reflecting Christ's rejection, the Damned are pushed and carried, and tumble toward the region of Hell at bottom left, in the first archivolt.[1] Surface abrasions have destroyed much of the detail in the upper portion of Christ's right sleeve. The shiny mortar of the very crude joining for the inset replacing the upper half of the soul on Christ's

FIG. 17.   Judging Christ, no. X, keystone, first archivolt

FIG. 18.   Angel no. IX presenting soul to Christ, first archivolt, center, left

FIG. 19. Detail, feet of angel no. XI presenting soul to Christ, first archivolt, center, right

right also covers portions of his sleeve. With those exceptions, the bust of Christ retains its twelfth-century surfaces. The well-preserved nimbus with its jeweled *croix-formée,* the delicately striated, twisted locks of hair on his left shoulder, most of the ornamented *galon* at the neck of his tunic, and the highly stylized draperies at the shoulder as well as the circular folds on his chest, all survive in excellent condition. The patterns created by the drapery conventions contrast with the striving for authenticity that inspired the meticulous detailing of the jewels in their elaborate settings on the *croix-formée* and on the *galon.* Yet the stylizations accord with the artistic attitudes of the Master of the Tympanum Angels.

ANGELS PRESENTING SOULS FOR JUDGMENT

Hovering on either side of the bust of Christ, two of the angels (nos. IX and XI, Figs. 18 and 19 and Plate Va), sent to "gather together his elect from the four winds, from the farthest parts of the heavens to the utmost bounds of them" (Matthew 24:31), present souls to Christ for judgment.[2] From the waist up, the bodies of the two souls are nineteenth-century insets. Both appeal for mercy with the same prayerful gesture made by Suger at Christ's feet. Although in this instance no fragments authenticate the gestures, they seem reasonable in the context of the continuing text of St. Matthew, which contains Christ's dialogue with the Blessed and the Damned (Matthew 25:35–46).

Even though marred by a number of nineteenth-century insets, the angel on Christ's right (no. IX) retains not only the original pose but also many interesting twelfth-century details (Fig. 19 and Plate Vb). In addition to the usual

57

replacement of the head, other insets cross each wing along the masonry joint of the voussoirs and include a portion of both of his feet and of the left foot and ankle of the soul. An inset also restores the lower half of the angel's right sleeve.

The detailing of the feathers of the wings, the sickle-shaped, incised folds over the right shoulder, the remnants of a teardrop fold in the drapery over the abdomen, and the solid, squat proportions of the figures identify the hand of the Master of the Tympanum Angels; the hemline around the right foot and the complicated folds of the trailing sash prove his ability to vary details. In both figures, the drapery convincingly simulates the angels' rapid passage through the air as they return from "the farthest parts of the heavens." In the closely con-voluted hemline over the foot of angel no. IX and in the fluted edges of the flut-tering sash, the artist achieved an unusual degree of relief. The parallel folds of the sash have wider creases than is usual for this sculptor. With their sharper ridges the folds resemble flattened, open pleats.

Although renewed by two insets and heavy mortar along the eroded joints of the voussoirs, as well as by a new head, the angel on Christ's left (no. XI, Plate Vb) survived in even better condition than his companion. Similar details in the carving of the wings and drapery associate this figure with the same mas-ter. Especially characteristic are the long, rounded, closely repeated folds of the veil or sash, which sweep in a simple curve from the right shoulder across the torso. The sash terminates in the same stylized folds that activate the hemlines of the tympanum angels' scarves. Earlier photographs show the cascade of the sash reworked with mastic, but that nineteenth-century restoration has fallen away to reveal damaged but unrecut surfaces.[3] The mutilation begins as the drapery falls from the left side, continues down to the lower edge, and includes the central, symmetrical foldback of the fabric.

In the second pair, the unrestored feet of both the angel and the soul are of particular interest. The latter are shown with soles upturned and toes extended, in the manner observable in a small child sleeping on his stomach. The angel's feet, flattened and distorted, contrast with the more naturalistic rendering (Fig. 19).

The left sleeve of the angel also deserves special mention because it pro-vides a plausible example for the proper reconstruction of the sleeves of the censing angels directly above in the second archivolt (nos. XVI and XVII, Plate Vb). The sequence of gently rippling folds of the fabric on the sleeve of angel no. XI, although unquestionably weathered and softened, differs from the series of more stylized folds terminating with the incised teardrop forms so prevalent in the drapery of the tympanum angels. Reflecting the recurrent search for naturalism that preoccupied the artists of the central portal, the rippling and modulated folds of the sleeve emphasize the tension and pull of the angel's outstretched arm.

CENSING ANGELS

In the center of the second archivolt above the bust of the Judging Christ and below the symbols of the Trinity, two censing angels (nos. XVI and XVII, Plate Va–b) emerge from stylized clouds. The cloud formations connect them more closely with the "Son of man coming in the clouds of heaven" (Matthew 24:30) than with the Trinity above. Appropriate in either context, however, their dual relationship demonstrates the careful organization and interrelationship of iconographical details in the central portal. The very noticeable restorations to the head, hands and arms, and to the two censers have raised doubts about the original attributes.[4] Careful examination of the multiple joints of the repairs revealed the survival of a very small twelfth-century portion of the base of the censer held by the angel on the left (no. XVI). Not a part of the inset replacing most of the censer, that small fragment was carved from the twelfth-century stone of the voussoir. Authenticating the restoration, the original sliver also authenticates the iconography of this pair as restored.

Possibly because of extensive damage to the central portions of the two figures, rather large areas of the carved surfaces show recutting above the shoulders and thighs, as diagrammed. The surviving drapery of the upper half of the right angel's sleeve (no. XVII) reinforces the proposal that the drapery along the rest of the sleeve originally resembled that of angel no. XI below. Other features, notably the details of the wings, the stylized hem of the floating sash, and the strongly incised accents on the ridges of the folds over the left thigh of angel no. XVI link this pair both with the angels directly below and with the tympanum angels.

59

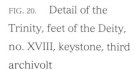

FIG. 20. Detail of the Trinity, feet of the Deity, no. XVIII, keystone, third archivolt

THE TRINITY

THE DEITY WITH THE APOCALYPTIC LAMB

The combined effect of nine insets and severely distorting recutting has completely destroyed the twelfth-century character of the Deity who, in the keystone of the third archivolt, holds a disk with the Agnus Dei (no. XVIII, Fig. 20 and Plate Vb). As the diagram indicates, the Deity's prominent face and his two feet belong to the nineteenth century. The devastating recutting of the lower drapery continues onto the adjacent surfaces of the voussoir, over which the drapery of the sleeves and lower edge of the tunic originally spread. The examination of the area suggests that the distorting modern feet transform what would have been a visually credible bust of God into a deformed dwarf. Yet sufficient evidence remains to verify the iconography of the figure of the Deity with a disk containing "the sign of the Son of man in heaven" (Matthew 24:30), and the validation of the feet as restored may lie in the iconography of the imagery rather than the archaeological evidence that appears to discredit them. Besides the problem of the aesthetically disfiguring feet, during the examination other questions arose concerning minor aspects of the repairs.

According to the Gospel of Matthew 24:30, the sign would be a precursor to the Son of man arriving in glory to judge—the image carved on the keystone of the first archivolt. Yet according to the Book of the Apocalypse, the Lamb in the midst of the twenty-four elders was to be the sign. The elders, crowned and carrying harps and vials, are represented here seated on thrones in the three outer archivolts (Apocalypse 5:8; Plates VIa–IXa). The vine enframing each of the elders in the fourth archivolt refers to the Tree of Jesse, the first representation in monumental sculpture of the tree depicting the genealogy of Christ. The inclusion of the vine adds a second meaning to the twenty-four figures by conflating the elders with the patriarchs of the Old Testament, who were the royal precursors of Christ.

The importance of the iconography of the Deity with the Agnus Dei and the questionable aspects of the restoration require an analysis in some detail. Two separate insets replace the upper left and right quadrants of the Deity's nimbus. The insets are bounded by the arms and stem of the recut *croix-formée*. The absence of jewels and ornamentation seems surprising, but no indications of twelfth-century embellishments remain.[5] The entire silhouette of the original head survives behind the new head. At the top, the fragment projects 1.5 cm. in front of the nimbus, and the line of joining gradually moves forward as it descends on both sides of the head, so that the original carving includes all the hair below the ears and on the shoulders. That unrecut remnant of the twelfth-century head and hair authenticates the proportions of the head in the nineteenth-century inset.

The disk and most of the Agnus Dei, as diagrammed (Plate Vb), are twelfth-century stone. The recutting of the disk proved especially severe in the upper right quadrant, where the surface was shaved back as much as 0.5 cm. Measured by the band of cut-back stone along the ridge of the spine and rump of the Lamb, the deep recutting also caused distortion at the perimeter of the disk in the same quadrant. The heavy recutting below the Lamb's chest removed all traces of his original left foot and foreleg, bent and raised in the traditional pose. The dowel scar in the stump of the leg indicates that the loss of the nineteenth-century replacement also caused the loss of some good twelfth-century carving. The original right foreleg still supports the twelfth-century foot of the cross. Its rounded stem raises a question about the shape of the cross proper in the nineteenth-century inset. Starkly unembellished, the square profile of the Latin cross as restored fails to continue the form of the stem visible today beneath the belly of the Lamb.

The body of the Lamb, the best-preserved twelfth-century carving in the ensemble, seems remarkable for its naturalism. The normal proportions, lifelike muzzle, cloven hooves, fetlock, and genitalia all give evidence of the artist's careful observation of nature. Yet he also drew on stylized conventions to depict the fleece, which he carved with delicately striated, evenly spaced, overlapping locks.

All the carved surfaces below the disk show recutting, and some of the flaring side folds as well as most of the sleeve drapery below the Deity's arms, especially under his right arm, were eliminated. The nineteenth-century restorer must have encountered severe damage that left illegible fragments of the drapery below the hands and disk. He could have misread the convolutions of the drapery along the lower edge of the voussoir and incorrectly interpreted ripples as indications for feet that never existed. Extensive surgery was necessary in order to insert them (Fig. 20). Directly below the disk, the figure of the Deity has been carved back so far that only the recut drapery over the insteps still projects beyond the original surface plane of the archivolt. Along the lower edge, between and around the nineteenth-century feet, as much as two-thirds of the original projection of the voussoir was cut away to accommodate them. They now lie entirely behind the original surface plane. In contrast to the modern feet, the projecting portion of the Deity's twelfth-century nimbus lies in part behind the surface plane but also projects prominently in front of it. Thus, in all four archivolts, only this figure has portions that both overlap the upper and lower edges and lie behind the background plane. And as restored, only this figure in the portal ensemble violates the aesthetic based on respect for the integrity of the human figure and natural proportions. The surgery required to insert the feet destroyed original carving, and their presence created a grotesque figure.

On the other hand, Gerson has proposed that cosmological schemata deriving from images of God the Creator holding a disk (symbolic of the cosmos) had in part inspired the image at Saint-Denis of God the Father with the disk framing the Lamb.[6] The *clipeus* is an attribute of glory, like a mandorla or a nimbus. The image of the Lamb in a *clipeus,* with foot raised supporting the staff of a cross, is not, as Schiller noted, "a straightforward symbol of the Passion, but rather the *signum Christi,* or symbol of victory."[7] Thus the image places emphasis on the Passion and the Lamb of God, which redeems all mankind, even as the symbolism of the *Agnus victor,* the apocalyptic Lamb within a disk held by the Deity in the midst of the elders, imbues the image with

FIG. 21. Dove with attendant angels, no. XIX, keystone, fourth archivolt

cosmic and universal significance. The dual meaning thus unites the imagery of Christ's Passion, his humanity, and its expiatory symbolism with the apocalyptic Second Coming, the eternal victory, and worldwide sovereignty understood in the image of the *signum Christi*.

In the 1973 French version of this study, the concept of the figure of God the Father with the disk and Lamb was not considered in connection with cosmic schemata. In such representations, the figure of God the Father is hidden behind the disk, with only his head, hands, and feet visible. Recent studies by Gerson, Zinn, and Rudolph interpreting the figure as being inspired by cosmic schemata seem to authenticate the feet as restored and explain the departure from the prevailing naturalism of the portal sculpture. Thus, despite the drastic measures the restorer took to insert feet and the resulting destruction of any authenticating archaeological evidence, their plausibility as part of a schema gives them credence. A cosmological interpretation of the imagery of God the Father holding a disk with the *signum Christi* seems perfectly consistent with Suger's preoccupation with symbolic modes of discourse, such as those that inform the programs of the windows and the gilt bronze doors of the central portal.

THE DOVE WITH TWO ANGELS

A nineteenth-century insertion but not a nineteenth-century invention, the Dove perches on a veil of stylized clouds held by two angels (no. XIX, Fig. 21 and Plate Vb). Although badly eroded, they survive nearly untouched by the restoration. Guilhermy's comment, "On a profité, m'a-t'on assuré, des moindres indications telles que les pattes de la colombe," validates the restoration of the Dove essential to the imagery of the Trinity.[8] The joint for the inset replacing the bird slices through the left angel's head and descends in a straight line that hugs the Dove's body and, passing around the tips of the leftmost claw of his right foot, moves into the middle of the ridge of the lowest large fold of the veil. Angling to the right across the ridge of that fold and following its curve, the joint then rises on the right side to bisect the left thumb of the right angel and ascends close to the Dove's left foot. After rounding that clawed foot, the line of joining turns left, back toward the bird, and pursues an upward course between the Dove and the angel on the right. The upper boundary of the inset lies in the surface plane behind the freestanding fan of tail feathers. Although the thickness of the crust on the eroded stone made a thorough brushing unfeasible, spot-testing suggested that the veil had not been recut.

Even though heavy soot and surface decay coat the figures of the angels in this most exposed location and obscure them, the hand of the Master of the Tympanum Angels as their carver seems probable. Despite the weathering, those unrecut figures retain their twelfth-century details. The sleeve drapery of the angel on the left has the character and broad sweep of the leg drapery of the upper tympanum angels (nos. II–V, Plate IIa–b), and traces of incised accents on the ridges of folds emerge through the surface decay on the sleeve. The feet of both archivolt angels echo the broad, twisted, and flattened feet of the angel in the first archivolt, to the right of the bust of Christ (angel no. XI, Fig. 19 and Plate Va). The less legible sleeve drapery of the angel to the right of the Dove displays the more archaic drapery convention of encircling folds that accent and identify joints. As the drapery of the veil supporting the Dove curves over the shoulder of the left angel, the cloudlike folds seem to condense into forms reminiscent of the scarves and veils of the tympanum angels. Although severely weathered, the surfaces of the wings also follow established patterns.

An inset replaces the face of the right angel. Except for a possible inset replacing the left angel's nose, however, no lines of joining could be discovered that would signal an inset replacing his head or face. Probably modern, that nose prevents the figure from being the single exception in the central portal to Didron's anguished report that "pas une pierre n'échappa à la main des ouvriers."[9] The nineteenth-century head of the Deity below, with his broad fore-head, spreading nose, full, flat lips, and huge protruding eyeballs rimmed with wide bands representing eyelids, seems an inept parody of the stylized face of this angel. After selective brushing, the drapery of the angels appeared untouched by the hand of the restorer, although surface corrosion may mask recut areas.

CHAPTER 5

THE DAMNED AND THE BLESSED
OF THE FIRST ARCHIVOLT

THE DAMNED AND THE TORTURES OF HELL

The scenes on the right, or south, side of the first archivolt (nos. XII–XV, Plates VIIIa and IXa) show the Damned and the tortures of Hell. An inscription incised into the outer beveled edge of the seven lower voussoirs reads: "S. J. BRUN, SCULPT. ELEVE DE LEMOT RESTAURA CE PORTAIL EN 1839." In this century, Brun's signature has invariably been interpreted as proof that the entire portion of the inner archivolt, left, is a nineteenth-century invention. Yet the examination authenticated numerous twelfth-century details and confirmed Guilhermy's report: "Il restait quelques indications qu'on a suivies."[1]

Twelve voussoirs contain the scenes of the Damned carved on their surfaces. Of those twelve, eight retain fragments of twelfth-century carving that guided Brun. Only the fourth, fifth, sixth, and seventh voussoirs from the bottom have scenes composed entirely of nineteenth-century insets. Of those, the figures on the fourth and seventh voussoirs follow the indications of twelfth-century fragments in the adjacent third and eighth voussoirs.

Seen from below, the turmoil of twisting bodies has the unmistakable appearance of a nineteenth-century restoration. Carved in four sections, the insets into those four voussoirs have joints that were easily identified from the scaffolding. Each nineteenth-century section was set with dowels and mortar in the original voussoir where a channel had been cut, which functioned as a mortise made to receive a tenon. As the diagram shows, in the fifth voussoir the inset also replaced the upper right section of the surface plane of the old stone. The restoration extends over to and includes some of the beveling along the outer edge.

The scenes of the Damned and Hell should be read from top to bottom: In the uppermost group (no. XII, Fig. 22 and Plate IXa), an angel is pushing a man-

FIG. 22. Angel no. XII, first archivolt, right, fourth tier, detail, scenes of the Damned

acled soul away from Judgment and down toward the region of Hell (Plate VIIIa). Despite some distortion caused by repairs to the masonry joint as it crosses the angel's left knee, portions of the best-preserved drapery carving of the entire portal survive in the lower part of the figure. Recutting eliminated the lowest fold on the angel's left thigh and reduced the dimensions of the knee. Once perfectly symmetrical, the drapery over the two thighs still has a beautifully spaced series of curving folds of the type associated with Languedoc. Reflecting the motion implicit in the pose of the figure, the drapery of the tunic flares out above and between the lower legs in a series of pleats. The complicated hemline terminates each pleat in an intricate cluster of foldbacks. The angel's bony feet grip the surface plane; the crouched pose becomes anatomically plausible when read as an arrangement perpendicular to the surface of the voussoir block. With the restorations, the angel appears considerably foreshortened when viewed from below.

As diagrammed (Plate IXb), the recut areas include the surface of the under edge of the angel's right wing. Possibly a break occasioned the recutting, for the loss of the tip seems to have reduced the wing enough to make it appear somewhat undersized. Despite the damage repaired by nineteenth-century insets, as indicated in the diagram, this angel survives as a notable example of the style and quality of the original sculpture of the portal.[2]

Still visible on the stomach of the damned soul pushed by the angel, a fragment of the original chain authenticates the manacles around her wrists. The unrestored arrangement of the hair and her maidenly breasts establish the sex of this doomed soul. The inset repairing her legs not only follows the dictates of the twelfth-century torso, but also connects with the original ankles carved from the voussoir directly below. Diminished only by light recutting near her left ear, the long, curling locks that reach to her waist survive from the original sculpture as a fine example of a twelfth-century coiffure for maidens.

The inset restoring the demon and the soul below in scene no. XIII follows the dictates of a generous vestige of the twelfth-century demon (Plate IXb). The original carving includes enough of his upper left arm to authenticate its raised position. Easily traced in its downward diagonal through his head and torso to the groin, the joining of the old and new stone then continues inconspicuously between the demon's thighs. A second inset forms the outer face of his left thigh and hip. The original left knee and lower leg survive, together with both twelfth-century feet. Clawed, with four birdlike toes, the feet probably provided the model for the hands and feet of the nineteenth-century demons below. A small, fleshy wing with large fish-scales over its surface sprouts from the demon's left heel. Except for that wing and the right foot below it, the extant twelfth-century surfaces all show some recutting. But the original fragments validate the pose and proportions of the demon which, together with his off-center placement, presuppose the second figure, which is most reasonably reconstructed as a damned soul whom the demon is dragging toward Hell.

Directly below, another twelfth-century fragment determined the placement and inverted position of the uppermost soul in group no. XIV (Plate VIIIb). Perfectly preserved, the right leg with foot kicking above the head of the demon joins the nineteenth-century figure at the groin. Notable for the modeling that articulates the bone structure of the knee and the musculature of the inner thigh, that leg has the same anatomically correct, rounded forms observed in the Resurrection frieze. The proportions of the leg demand a figure approximating the size of the restored body, and the pose presumes what the restoration has provided—a demon who is carrying a soul slung carelessly over his shoulder.

The beak-faced devil below and the two souls in his clutches have no authenticating twelfth-century vestiges, nor has the small soul carried by a demon on the right, directly above the crenellated parapet (nos. XIV and XV, Plate VIIIb). But on the left, the demon leaning over the parapet continues the activity assigned him by the surviving portion of his right arm hauling on the rope, also original, with which he is strangling the soul in torment below.

As the diagram shows, much of the original architecture of Hell survives as well as most of the soul in Hell and her tormenters: demons, viper, toad, and winged monsters. The left side of the building, the demon's arm, and even the rope escaped recutting. Elsewhere recutting proved negligible, except above the body of the lower winged beast on the right. There the wall of the building has been cut back so severely that none of the original surface carving survives. The wings of the beast also appear to be considerably reduced in size. All other insets follow the requirements of the twelfth-century sculpture, except for the grotesque faces in the left lancet. Yet they seem acceptable restorations, since they compare well with the original face peering out of the right lancet from beneath the belly of the monster. The notably well-preserved, coiled tail of that monster terminates in still another small face—an original conceit that has survived in good condition.

The lively tangle of tormenters at the foot of the wall creates the same kind of turbulence found above in the twelfth- and nineteenth-century arrangement of intertwined bodies. The turmoil of the lower composition gives additional credence to the not fully authenticated nineteenth-century portions. In the twelfth-century group, the viper coiled around the soul's right foot and the winged beast attacking from the opposite side seem to be pulling her limb from limb. The toad attacking her genitals adds the ultimate agony to her eternal torment. The lightly modeled figure of the soul, anatomically explicit and naturally proportioned, seems comparable in every way to the figures of the Resurrected Dead in the lintel zone (Fig. 11 and Plates IIIa and IVa). Lively and realistic, with feet twisted and braced, the agonized contortions of her legs reflect the several tortures she is suffering.

PARADISE, THE BLESSED, AND THE FIFTH WISE VIRGIN

In contrast to the turmoil and disorder of the scenes of Hell, the scenes of Paradise, located on the inner archivolt to Christ's right, divide into three serene and discrete groups (nos. 5 and VI–VIII, Figs. 23 and 24 and Plates IIIa, VIa, and VIIa). Although critics have questioned the authenticity of that disparity, the examination of the scenes of Hell discussed above indicated that the continuous group of souls and demons tumbling into Hell retain at least the original outlines. In the feudal world of the twelfth century, order clearly symbolized

69

FIG. 23. Detail of the Archangel "Gabriel" carrying souls, no. VII, first archivolt, left, second tier

the state of the elect, whereas disorder was the fate of the outcast. The literal representation of those contrasting conditions in the first archivolt provides additional evidence of a preoccupation with didactic imagery in the Saint-Denis portal program.

The identification of the three heavenly scenes as well as their relative positions on the archivolt depend on passages in the gospels according to St. Luke and St. Matthew. Standing in the lintel zone of the tympanum near the open Gate to Paradise in the lowest tier, the fifth Wise Virgin (no. 5, Plate IIIa) is ready to go in with the bridegroom to the marriage (Matthew 25:10)—the metaphor for

Paradise and the destination of the Blessed.[3] Three of the elect have already entered through the gate (no. VI, Plate VIa). One stands in the open door; the other two are carried by angels. Directly above that group, an angel is holding two souls (no. VII, Fig. 23 and Plate VI). Perhaps he represents the Archangel Gabriel who stood before God (Luke 1:19), or possibly he is the unnamed angel who carried Lazarus to his eternal reward, since the third group depicts Abraham with three souls in his bosom (no. VIII, Fig. 24 and Plate VII). Another metaphor for Paradise, that imagery rests on the parable of the rich man Dives and the beggar Lazarus. Dives, "clothed in purple and fine linen . . . [had] feasted sumptuously every day," but had shown no kindness toward the starving Lazarus, "who lay at his gate full of sores." When they both died, Dives went to hell, but Lazarus "was carried by an angel into Abraham's bosom" (Luke 17:19–22).

The lowest, or first scene, showing the open gate and the Blessed within the Heavenly City, seems particularly interesting because of the architecture. In addition, the small nude figures, metaphorical representations of the human soul, provide a stylistic link with the figures of the Resurrected Dead in the lintel zone and with the soul in torment in Hell. As diagrammed (Plate VIb), the insets restoring the figures of the Blessed proved routine and noncontroversial in that they perpetuated the original arrangements. The positions of the four nineteenth-century heads accord with the alignments of the torsos and shoulders, but as usual, the facial style detracts from the visual effect. Except for the original but heavily recut face of the soul standing in the doorway, the recutting appeared light enough to be deemed negligible.

The architectural details that deserve special mention include the hardware of the doors, the depiction of mortar so heavily applied that it oozes out of the masonry joints in the abutments of the large lancets on the left, and the ornamental zigzag occupied by circles that surrounds the lancet—all realistic renderings based on observations. Then, in an unexpected reversion to stylization, the artist ornamented the stepped-back buttress on the left with rows of incised triangles—an architectural fantasy amusing for its juxtaposition with such accurate details as the pins of the horseshoe-shaped hinges upon which the gate swings. Although they are heavily encrusted and no longer sharply defined, similar triangles in series ornament the architecture of some of the baldachins above the Wise and Foolish Virgins on the jambs of the portal below.

71

Such small details help to forge the links between the sculpture of the inner archivolt and the figures on the left and right jambs—all attributable to the Angel Master (see Chapter 6).

The delicately modeled torso of the soul carried by the angel on the left reflects the same attitudes toward the human body, expressed in the lively, realistic figures of the Resurrected Dead. Although anatomically explicit, the figure of the soul filling the doorway to Paradise appears flatter, and the proportions seem less credible. Yet features common to the sculpture of the inner archivolt, jambs, and Resurrection frieze suggest that one artist, the Master of the Tympanum Angels, was responsible for all those iconographically related figures. The stylized drapery of the angels of the Heavenly City, although skimpy, also seems compatible with the drapery of the other archivolt angels, and their wings have the same form and characteristics as the wings carved by him; his hand and ideas seem to dominate those groups.

The Angel Master left his stylistic signature more prominently in the drapery of the Archangel "Gabriel" above, who is carrying two of the elect (no. VII, Fig. 23). As diagrammed (Plate VIb), a single inset replaced the upper portion of the angel as well as the torsos and heads of the two souls in his arms. Insets that once restored the toes on both of his feet have fallen away. Except along the hem, the original drapery shows no recutting and only negligible weathering. Every crease of the folds in the drapery across his torso ends in a teardrop-shaped depression. The artist, emphasizing the intricate patterns of the draperies, outlined the terminus of each depression by incising a line on the ridges of the folds. Generously spaced hook folds curve alternately from left to right down and across the angel's tubular legs. The bold vertical pleats in series framing his legs assist in the definition of their solid, unsubtle forms. The angel has the same short, stocky proportions that characterize the figures of the tympanum angels. The combination of drapery elements in the lower half of the figure expresses in broader terms the same conventions defining the **V** of the groin and thighs of the tympanum angel no. V (Plate IId). In the upper half of the "Gabriel" figure, the arrangement includes teardrop folds that help to locate his hands beneath the veil. Widely spaced, concentric **U**-shaped folds below his right hand and again below his right forearm have the Languedocian incised lines accenting the ridges. On both sides of the figure the scarf falls with deeply undercut, thick, folded-back edges. The heavy folds that circle below his

FIG. 24.   Abraham with three souls in his bosom, no. VIII, first archivolt, left, third tier

left forearm swirl around his hand in a pattern reminiscent of the highly stylized right-knee drapery of angel no. XII in the scenes of the Damned (Fig. 22). Bolder, perhaps, with strongly stated curves and reverse curves, the arrangement underscores the forward projection of the forearm cradling the figure of the soul. In contrast with that highly stylized encircling drapery, the soul rests his tiny hand on the angel's arm in the easy, affectionate manner of a small child held in a mother's arms—the same gesture made by the soul on the left in the scene below.

The heavy, squat figure of Abraham occupies the third tier in the scenes of the Blessed (no. VIII, Fig. 24 and Plate VIIa). The stunted arms and foreshortened thighs exaggerate the stocky proportions so evident in the "Gabriel" figure below, and they are also typical of the other figures attributable to the Master of the Tympanum Angels. Bonded at a masonry joint, the inset for

73

Abraham's modern head includes both shoulders and small portions of the decorated *galon* at the neck of his tunic. The heads of the three small souls in his bosom also belong to the nineteenth century. As diagrammed (Plate VIIb), other insets replace part of the lower portion of the hammock formed by the scarf, three toes of his right foot, and the tip of the scarf falling from his right hand. Slight recutting has affected the surfaces adjacent to the largest inset in the veil, the area along his left side below the left hand, and also most of the bench on the same side. The rest of the figure, although corroded by the weather and pollution, retains its original surfaces. Most of the minor repairs in mortar on the ridges of the folds of the lap drapery have crumbled and fallen away.

An original, small, delicately proportioned hand pokes out from beneath the chin of the soul on the right side of Abraham's bosom. That structurally accurate hand rests on the unnaturally thick edge of the scarf. The hammock formed by the scarf seems much too small to contain the three bodies presumed to occupy it. Paradoxically, the solid reality of the bulging swag and of the squat figure of Abraham is achieved by the interplay of curves created by a profusion of much-repeated, highly stylized folds. The multifold scarf caught up by Abraham's outstretched hands forms a festoon, and teardrop-shaped folds crease the scalloped loop of the scarf clutched in his right hand. Concentric folds with incised accents on the ridges define his lap from knee to knee and form a second festoon, which is completed by the fall of pleats on either side of the legs. The high-ridged, deeply creased side pleats differ from the less typical side pleats with fluted ridges flanking the legs of "Gabriel" below (no. VII, Fig. 23). Even more than in the recut hem of the latter, the pleats in Abraham's tunic flatten into ripples along the hem. In both figures, the hemline between the feet and the folded-back edges of the veils have the closed formation of the central foldback associated with the Master of the Tympanum Angels. Well-preserved concentric folds define Abraham's lower left leg. With the concentric folds between the legs and the incised hook folds on the right shin, the multifolds by their very profusion mask the distortingly stumpy proportions of his legs and the minimal projection of his knees. Among the seated figures of the archivolts, this figure has no stylistic parallel.

Abraham's footrest with its especially succulent leaves shares an arrangement with the foliage of the two scenes below. Based on a repetition in tiers of a palmette motif, their plan differs from the centrally organized foliate designs that prevail in the patriarchs' consoles (Figs. 33 and 34). Although variations on the palmette motif in the outer archivolts seem endless, the homogeneous organization of the foliate ornament below the three scenes of Paradise suggests a deliberate repetition of an arrangement in order to unify the scenes visually, and certainly points to the work of an artist other than the one responsible for the patriarchs (see Chapter 7). Along its base, Abraham's footrest has a continuous roll of compact scrolls, a modified version of the classical continuous-scroll motif. That minute decoration provides the only occurrence in the sculpture of the central portal of an abstract motif based on a classical or Antique pattern.[4] The foliage of "Gabriel's" footrest rises from a torus decorated with an arcade formed by leaves—another interesting and unusual ornamental detail.

The photographic detail of the restored tiers of foliage that form the footing for the Heavenly City (no. VI, Fig. 7) provides a perfect example of the techniques of the restoration and the deterioration caused by weather along the joints of insets. As described above, a comparison of the detail of the photograph with the diagram (Plate VIb) reveals discernible differences between the textures of the twelfth-century stone and the modern insets, as well as the surface modification in the old stone caused by even the lightest recutting.

CHAPTER 6

THE JAMB SCULPTURES WITH THE PARABLE OF THE TEN VIRGINS

THE WISE AND FOOLISH VIRGINS AND THE TWO ATLANTIDS

The Wise and Foolish Virgins on the two jambs and in the lintel zone (nos. 1–5, 6–10) present the most complicated and puzzling archaeological problems of the central portal. Vulnerable because of their location, at least partially dismantled and reassembled in the restorations of 1770–1771, fractured and patched, the sculptures today show the combined effects of wear, manipulation, shifting stresses, mutilations, and two campaigns of restoration.[1] Often we can distinguish between the eighteenth- and nineteenth-century restorations because the earlier restorer proves more respectful of and *simpatico* with the twelfth-century work; thus his insets are less discordant than those carved by Brun. The earlier restorer also used plaster of Paris for repairs, which he protected with weather-resistant mastic. The plaster is crumbling away where the surface coating has chipped or scaled. The generous applications of mastic also partially mask the joints around insertions, as well as numerous cracks and some horizontal cuts made to facilitate the temporary removal of some of the virgins during the dismounting of the jambs. As the diagrams indicate, the restorations have created a confusing maze of insets in the sculpture—repairs that frequently include some of the surrounding masonry. The insets fall into two categories: first, those that remedy damage to a figure and its surround; and second, as noted earlier (see Chapter 2), the *couvres-joints* that repair and mask eroded masonry joints where they impinged upon the sculpture. Both the identification and significance of all insets in the jambs depended to a large degree on an understanding of the twelfth-century system of masonry construction of the portals. As also described in Chapter 2, beginning with the fifth

FIG. 25a.   Foolish Virgin
no. 6 and Atlantid no. 6a,
right jamb, lowest tier

FIG. 25b.   Detail, diagram
of restorations to head of
Foolish Virgin no. 6

horizontal bed, the stones of the portals measure 29.5 cm. Any deviation of more
than 0.5 cm. from that norm invariably indicated a repair or *couvre-joint.*[2]

Differentiating between the *couvres-joints* and the eighteenth- and
nineteenth-century stone repairs that also interrupt the masonry joints was complicated by the generous application of a protective coating, particularly noticeable over the surfaces of the lower figures. On the right jamb, the coating
hardened into a shell-like surface through which the details of the twelfth-
century carving remain visible (see especially Foolish Virgin no. 6, Fig. 25a). On
the more weathered left, or north jamb, the chemicals of air pollutants seem
to have attacked the coating and reduced it to a thick, heavily wrinkled skin or
encrustation. The wrinkling proved especially troublesome in the analysis of
restorations to the figures of Wise Virgins nos. 1 and 2. Because identification
of recutting of twelfth-century carving depended as much on surface textures
and stone color as on the character of the carving, only the most heavily recut
areas could be positively identified. Wherever the coating prevailed, any
subtler and lighter retouching was undetectable beneath the weathered mastic. Under such circumstances the analysis of surface conditions became more

77

tentative than usual, and therefore the text, rather than the diagrams, will note recut areas along with descriptions of what has survived of value where the protective coating proved most opaque.

A look at the photographs of the jambs (Figs. 6a–b, Plates X and XI), reminds us of the regular joints of the twelfth-century system governing the masonry of the embrasures and jambs. On both sides of the portals, the joints of the horizontal beds of stone can also be followed as they extend behind the nineteenth-century columns that replaced the lost statue-columns.[3] The insets that form a patchwork of repairs in the lower figures of the right jamb, Foolish Virgin and Atlantid, nos. 6 and 6a, best demonstrate the problems of the restorations and the importance of the masonry system in their resolution.

Besides providing a key to the identification of insets, the masonry system also helped to correct a longstanding error. The masonry joint of the upper edge of the sixth horizontal bed where it crosses the shoulders of Foolish Virgin no. 6 has been consistently mistaken for the joining of an inset. Earlier observers described the entire head as a nineteenth-century restoration, although the facial style and hair alone distinguish it from the restored heads of the other virgins.[4] The loosened triangular wedge of plaster of Paris that repaired the hair above the left shoulder provided additional evidence corroborating a twelfth-century date for some of the head. Newly exposed in 1968 because of the failed bonding, the surfaces showed all the characteristics of the twelfth-century limestone. In addition, the fluent lines of the striated hair, which curve to reveal the fully rounded, well-formed head, contrast strikingly with the hair of the nineteenth-century heads. The modern hair fits the head and stands away from the neck as stiffly as an English barrister's wig (see especially Wise Virgin no. 4, Plate Xa–b). The examination in the late 1960s and early 1970s seemed to indicate that the entire head of Foolish Virgin no. 6 had survived from the twelfth century, as stated in the article of 1973 analyzing restorations to the central portal.[5] In 1984, after eleven more years of weathering and attrition, a new look at the head produced evidence that has modified the earlier conclusions. The new evidence indicated that the hair immediately framing the face as well as the face itself belong to the restorations of 1770–1771, as diagrammed (Fig. 25b). The eighteenth-century hair and face continue the forms established by the twelfth-century head, but in front of the joint attaching the modern portion, the striations become somewhat coarser and more widely spaced.

The damages still visible on the face apparently were not deemed serious enough for a nineteenth-century replacement, and the restoration was then confined to the lost mortar patch at the back of the neck.

The eighteenth-century face has a charm absent from the restored faces of the next century. Foolish Virgin no. 6, looking down and to the left as dictated by the twelfth-century portion of her bowed head, has an easy grace as she stares at her empty lamp. She stands in a reflective pose, her head framed by the recess beneath the baldachin. Only the head and lamp project beyond the surface plane of the jamb, in contrast with her figure, which seems flattened and somewhat distorted because the feet and legs follow the demands of the inward slant of the masonry above the plinth (Plate XIa). The volume and projection of the head express two important qualities that distinguish the nascent Gothic style from the Romanesque. Yet with such contrasting artistic ideas in a single figure, it is small wonder that observers relegated the entire head to another period. Notably, in all the figures of virgins the degree of projection and undercutting increases from hem to shoulder, and originally the salience of their heads beneath the canopies reflected the new aesthetic.

Uncertainties surround the dates at which certain changes and excisions occurred in the jambs, nor are the reasons for all the alterations clear. For instance, some but not all of the niches that frame the virgins have been made narrower (see virgins nos. 2 and 3, Plate Xb). Although the insets repairing columns, capitals, and baldachins in those altered aedicules obviously date from the nineteenth century, the reasons for the changes, if they also date from that time, remain obscure. Another alteration affected the height of the jambs. The baldachins above virgins nos. 7 and 9 have been cut off, so that only small fragments or stumps at the springing of the arches remain. Since the 1770–1771 alterations increased rather than decreased the size of the portal, cropping the baldachins would have had the wrong result. The fact that portions are missing seems more explicable in terms of difficulties encountered in the original assemblage of the sculptural ensemble than as a later alteration.[6] Such an explanation presupposes that the jamb sculptures were not carved in situ, but rather in the workshop. A miscalculation or even a last-minute modification of the original plan could have necessitated the cropping of the uppermost baldachins.

An additional alteration in the original design occurred on the right jamb where the vertical rinceau bordering the niches ceases abruptly at the top of the second niche. In addition, above that point the masonry immediately to the right of the niches becomes idiosyncratic and confused, even though it still conforms to the regular horizontal beds of the twelfth-century masonry system. Although the aberrations are difficult to explain, either in terms of the alterations made in 1770–1771 or as an aspect of the nineteenth-century restorations, they could represent another adaptation to difficulties encountered at the time of assemblage and installation of the sculpture.[7] Yet the narrowing of the niches, like the elimination of the vertical rinceau, would have increased the width of the doorway and thus could date from 1771. The cropping of the baldachins that reduced the height of the jambs seems less irrational when considered in terms of the great bronze doors, commissioned by Suger, that were cast for the central portal. Perhaps the dimensions of the finished valves failed to accord with the specifications for the jambs—measurements that had governed the planning and execution of the sculpture. Alterations in the jambs could have made the necessary accommodations to those discrepancies, whereas changing the dimensions of the bronze doors would have been extremely difficult.

Other arrangements in the altered niches also strongly suggest changes made prior to the nineteenth-century restorations. Although the evidence fails to certify a twelfth-century date for them, reconstructing the conditions and idiosyncracies of the jambs with which the restorer had to contend proved helpful in understanding the existing arrangements. For example, the off-center, asymmetrical baldachin above Wise Virgin no. 3 consists principally of a nineteenth-century inset. As the diagram shows, only portions of the left turret survive from the twelfth century (Plate Xb). The right turret was sacrificed when the niche was made narrower. If vestiges of the right tower had survived to the time of the restoration, or if the restorers had been responsible for the narrowing of the niche, we could reasonably expect the restoration to provide a balanced architectural superstructure having turrets on both sides of the dome. We may safely assume that the inset perpetuated an existing asymmetry. The vertical cut to the right of the same virgin's body must also date from the earlier alteration, for it pinpoints the areas excised to make the width of the niche consonant with the narrower baldachin. On the other side of the figure there is still ample space between her body and the frame. Wise Virgin no. 2, directly below, also appears to be squeezed by the column on her left, and again

the baldachin shows signs of accommodation to a niche narrower than originally intended. The somewhat lopsided canopy arches above the figure and
rests on the outer, or right half of the abacus of the right capital. The other
half of the abacus projects into the recess formed by the canopy. Once again
the alterations must have preceded the nineteenth-century restoration, since
the abacus and capital, both part of a nineteenth-century inset, follow the
requirements of the twelfth-century column they surmount. Then, too, the
twelfth-century column and baldachin, except for the generous layers of protective coating, appear unaffected by the restorations. Again, the inset apparently perpetuated an existing architectural anomaly.

In sum, although surrounded with uncertainties, the attempts to reconstruct
the physical conditions that obtained before the restorations help to differentiate
between the work done earlier and modifications attributable to the nineteenth
century. Every stone in the jambs has been examined and every shred of evidence
evaluated. Yet not every aberration has a sure explanation, nor can every con-
tradiction be resolved with a verifiable hypothesis. Only by once again dis-
mantling the much-abused jambs would all the questions raised by the anomalies
be answered. Some of the secrets of the virgins probably lie hidden under
mortar and cement which, in turn, are coated with mastic and grime. Yet asymmetry and deformations still notify the viewer of modifications to the original plan.

Despite uncertainties about the chronology or sequence of alterations, the
detailed examination of the sculpture resulted in a number of conclusions
concerning the accuracy of the restoration, the characteristics of the twelfth-
century style, and the original appearance of the figures of the virgins in their
niches as well as that of the two Atlantids supporting the jamb colonnettes.

The insets replacing the heads and arms of both Atlantids and most of
the torso of Atlantid no. 1a rank among the most inept and distorting of the
nineteenth-century work. The tiny, malformed arms and hands, incapable of
bearing any weight, probably resulted from a misunderstanding of surviving
fragments, if any, that might have guided the restorer. The original arrangements may have paralleled that of the Atlantid of the western portal of the
duomo in Piacenza, who supports the twin columns below the statue of Adam.
With arms raised and bent as they cross above his slightly protruding head, the
Piacenza Atlantid bears the weight of the load on his elbows and forearms.[8]

81

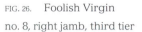

FIG. 26.   Foolish Virgin
no. 8, right jamb, third tier

Except for the new head and the heavy mortar filling the masonry joint across the legs, the figure of Foolish Virgin no. 8 appears quite unspoiled by the restoration (Fig. 26). Despite her weathered and worn surfaces, she best demonstrates how the virgins once looked beneath their canopies. Although lightly recut on the surface of the right turret, the baldachin provides a splendid example of the architecture of the turreted canopies.[9] Penetrating the darkness of the recess, lancets and oculi pierce the towers, turrets, and gables.

The spatial reality of those architectural elements enhances the forward projection of the fully undercut baldachin. Erring in the restoration of the aedicule of Wise Virgin no. 3 (Plate Xb), the restorer provided it with the only baldachin above the first tier that does not attain a comparable degree of projection. As a result, Wise Virgin no. 3 seems crowded beneath her canopy. The six upper figures under canopies all project forward and thereby represent a major departure from the Romanesque respect for the surface plane (see Figs. 6a–b). Gone also is the frontal Romanesque figure centered under an arch. No longer do the contours of the frame determine the proportions of the figures. Quite short but still credibly proportioned, the virgins exist in the three-dimensional space created by their architectural frames.

No surgery has altered the spatial relationship of figure to frame for Foolish Virgin no. 8. Placed somewhat off center and turned slightly to the left, she stands with firm footing on a grotesque monster whose forward projection at least equals that of the baldachin above. Hunched and contorted, he reaches back over his head to grab at her feet. His pointed ears, leering grimace, and pose seem characteristic of twelfth-century Dionysian animal fantasies.[10] Only the loss of a portion of the scarf or cloth falling from the virgin's right hand has affected the way in which the figure originally filled the space. The broken surfaces beneath her hand and the jagged fragment on her right hip indicate that the lost portion of the scarf was fully undercut—a technical detail that would have enhanced the general sense of form and volume and underscored the extent to which the right hand projects beyond the frame. The turn of her left shoulder gives the impression that she is leaning against the right column. The flutter of the hem seems like a minor infraction of the frame, but the figure as a whole represents a major change in artistic attitudes.

In that same figure, the unusually fluid lower folds of the garment respond to the contours of her feet and spread across the rump of the monster. Alongside her right foot, the back hemline shows below the same thick, convoluted edges of the front hem. That inner or back hemline, so characteristic of Dionysian drapery, occurs in every figure on the jambs except Foolish Virgin no. 9 (Plate XIa–b) directly above, where heavy recutting apparently eliminated every trace of it. The interplay of curves, another preoccupation of the Master of the Tympanum Angels, enlivens the drapery of virgin no. 8 and seems especially important and effective in the drapery arrangements of virgins nos. 1, 2, 3, and 6 and Atlantid no. 6a. Too little remains of the drapery of Atlantid no. 1a to make a valid stylistic analysis. Yet the arrangement of his loin drapery resembles that of his opposite number, whose closely spaced, concentric, U-shaped folds still have traces of an incised line accenting each ridge. Shadowy outlines of that stylization also survive on the ridges of the concentric folds that arch across the torso of Foolish Virgin no. 8. The motif appears in every other jamb figure except virgin no. 7 (Plate XIb), whose drapery, worn, recut, and coated on the surfaces, is now merely a parody of the original arrangement, especially in the upper half of the body. The highly stylized, circular fold that defines the left breast of virgin no. 8 also accents those of the other jamb figures (see virgins nos. 3, 6, 7, and 9). There, too, as in the draperies of the Master of the Tympanum Angels, we find other variants on the drapery convention that encircles and pinpoints joints (virgins nos. 3 and 6).

The drapery arrangement defining the legs of virgin no. 8 recurs with variations in all the jamb figures. The long fall of pleats beside and between her legs terminates in a convoluted hemline, and the concentric U-shaped folds, sometimes abbreviated into a curving hook, arch over the thighs and loop across the shins. On the virgin's right leg, the folds appear to form an oval encircling the smooth, rounded ridge of the thigh and knee—another favorite convention in the stylistic vocabulary of the Master of the Tympanum Angels. This exemplar of the Wise and Foolish Virgins also has the crumpled sleeve, the pointed shoe, ornamented cuff, and jeweled clasp—familiar twelfth-century details, but all somewhat weathered and worn.

Despite the virgins' many common characteristics, the sculptor took pains to differentiate each one in dress, pose, and in his handling of shared drapery elements, and, as the surviving evidence suggests, in headdress and hairstyle as well. Almost every canopy, niche, and figure contains some detail of particular interest, such as the swirl or loop of material that virgin no. 8 holds in her hand, and the monster at her feet.

Such distinctive details merit at least passing mention. Although badly worn and heavily coated with mastic, Wise Virgin no. 1 retains the outlines of especially lavish twelfth-century drapery distinguished by a profusion of folds. The closely repeated folds of her veil, mantle, sleeves, and tunic create a marvelously fluent and active linear pattern. The folds, so typical of the draperies of the Master of the Tympanum Angels, retain no traces of the characteristic teardrop terminations, but in these worn surfaces their survival would be surprising. The trefoil arch of her canopy, an unusual architectural feature, has a counterpart in the baldachin above Foolish Virgin no. 8, although the latter is three-dimensional. Beneath the coating, the canopy above virgin no. 1 still has the outlines of the masonry system of the walls, and the tiled roof of the central gable appears particularly well preserved.

In the recess of the aedicule, a significant iconographical detail has survived from the twelfth century. Carved in low relief on the surface plane above the nineteenth-century lamp, an irregular protrusion 4.5 cm. high and 1 cm. wide completes the nineteenth-century flame, which rises to the height of 2 cm. from the bowl of the restored lamp. A similar projection, smaller and visible only from above, rises in the center of the bowl of the lone surviving twelfth-century lamp carried by Wise Virgin no. 4. Probably also a remnant of the original flame, that raised node indicates that in the twelfth century, the Wise Virgins of Saint-Denis bore lighted lamps as they went in with the bridegroom to the marriage. The virgins at Saint-Denis accurately illustrate Christ's parable of the ten virgins, which he likened to the Kingdom of Heaven. But only five of them were prepared to enter. Of the ten who went out to meet the bridegroom and the bride, "five of them were foolish and five were wise . . . the five foolish, having taken their lamps, did not take oil with them: But the wise took oil in their vessels with the lamps" (Matthew 25:1–4).

The figure and niche of Wise Virgin no. 2 seem noteworthy for the striking similarities of the drapery from waist to ankle compared with the folds defining the hips, laps, and legs of tympanum angels nos. III–V (Plate IIc–d). Without question, the same hand is responsible for both figures. Also noteworthy and still visible through the heavily coated surfaces, a delicately traced geometric pattern ornaments the border of the virgin's garment and, like the spiral columns and geometric design on socles beneath their bases, enriches the ensemble. On the plinth supporting the niche, a favorite Dionysian design recurs, consisting of palmettes emerging from clasps that gather and hold the stem of the rinceau.[11] Another motif decorating the wall of the turreted canopy consists of a row of zigzags alternating with incised lines that follow diagonal rather than horizontal courses. The latter, a decorative stylization, contrasts with the quite realistic masonry on the baldachin below, as it did in the Gate to Paradise in the first archivolt.

Wise Virgin no. 3 (Plate Xa–b) stands on a fantastic beast which hangs from the plinth by its fore and hind paws. The body and foreleg have been so severely cut back that the forward projection of the beast does not approach that of the monster in the parallel niche on the opposite jamb (no. 8). The garments of virgin no. 3, almost a copybook arrangement of familiar drapery conventions, include a pleated scarf draped over the left shoulder. Its fluted, folded-back edge is repeated on a larger scale in the cloth clutched in her left hand, which falls in a cascade across her thigh and down her left side. In the active hemline of her gown, the inner edges underneath the prominent symmetrical foldback meet neatly at the center in the manner preferred by the Master of the Tympanum Angels. That detail also occurs in the hems of Wise Virgins nos. 1 and 4. Guilhermy reported that the figure of virgin no. 3 looked as though she had been worn away by rain ("collée par la pluie").[12] Today the comment still obtains, especially with reference to the left side of the torso and her left arm and hand. Nevertheless, the incised folds of the left sleeve and the circular folds defining the abdomen and left breast remain quite clear. With precocious naturalism, the sculptor modeled the contours of her breast but at the same time used the especially stylized convention of an encircling fold. The juxtaposition of those natural and stylized forms recurs in other figures on the jambs (see Foolish Virgins nos. 6, 7, and 9).

The uppermost figure on the left jamb, Wise Virgin no. 4, seems unexpectedly stiff and awkward in spite of the sense of motion her stance was intended to evoke. The loss of all the lower skirt drapery along her left side and the recutting of the figure from shoulder to toe detract tremendously from the effectiveness of the sculpture. In addition, the coarse carving of the nineteenth-century head and shoulders dominates the figure. The overwhelming volume and depth of that inset emphasize the badly deformed left shoulder. Yet despite overall recutting, elements of twelfth-century drapery survive in the hook folds defining the right leg, the incised folds of the left sleeve, and the stylized treatment of the lower left leg. Most of the inset replacing the left fingers has fallen away, but the left hand still shows a remarkable projection.[13] The disproportionately large hands, so startling in this figure, represent another characteristic shared by a majority of the virgins, whose bodies otherwise have quite normal proportions (see especially the twelfth-century hands of virgins nos. 6, 8, 9, as well as nos. 5 and 10 in the lintel zone, Plates IIIa and IVa).

86

In profile, the figures on the left jamb project increasingly in ascending order. A similar progression also occurs in the right jamb. Obviously no accident, the sculptor apparently tried to compensate for the steadily increasing distance of the figures from eye level. The same sophisticated formal progression occurs in the figures of the patriarchs in the archivolts, where the lower figures also appear flatter than the upper ones, and the depth of the surface modeling of richly patterned draperies generally increases in the higher locations.

Little survives of Wise Virgin no. 5, who approaches the Heavenly City from the lintel zone (Plate IIIb). Heavy recutting and three appallingly bad insets destroyed all but the rudiments of the twelfth-century pose. The crude inset that replaced her lower legs, together with recutting in depth from the waist down, caused the drapery below the hips to read as a series of lumps. Yet some of the grace and ease of the original pose survive in the interplay of curves and reverse curves along her right side from head to knee. Although the restorer deserves the ultimate blame for the present appearance of the virgin, the leftmost fracture of the lower stone of the tympanum wrought additional havoc as it passed through and bisected the figure vertically.

More remains of the twelfth-century sculpture in the figure of Foolish Virgin no. 10 at the opposite end of the lintel (Plate IVb), but only her hands, the lamp, the right side of her chest, and the trailing lock of hair above the right shoulder retain unretouched twelfth-century surfaces. Elsewhere, as diagrammed, insets and overall recutting prevail. In general the recutting simplified the drapery and reduced it to the basic schema. A vertical cut extending upward from the right end of the modern lintel stone bisects the lower half of her figure. Apparently made to implement the removal of the section of her figure directly above the new lintel, the surgical cut follows the horizontal of her shins, rounds the knees, and moves up between the adjacent sarcophagus and her right thigh, then curves to the right beneath her abdomen to meet the vertical cut. During the 1770–1771 restorations, that portion of the figure must have been removed to implement the replacement of the lintel stone. After it was in place, the excised portion of the figure of the virgin was reinserted and mortared securely. (A similar surgical cut running the length of Wise Virgin no. 1 must have facilitated the rebuilding of the lower left jamb.)

The pose of Foolish Virgin no. 10 appears unchanged, and the silhouette of the original head backs and informs the inset repairing her face and hair. The artist's characteristic attention to detail resulted in a splendid and noteworthy assortment of hardware for the closed Gate to Paradise on the virgin's right. She holds the circular handle of twisted metal. Directly above, a mighty bolt, lock plate, and clamp, marvelous in their accuracy, bar her way to Paradise, but they are scaled to a gate many times the size of this one.

Below, in the first niche of the right jamb, the figure of Foolish Virgin no. 6 (Fig. 25a) provides visual balance for her counterpart across the doorway. All four figures in the lowest rank are modeled in low relief, and except for the head and lamp of virgin no. 6, do not project beyond the surface plane of the jambs. Yet the profusion of the folds of their drapery gives the two virgins in the first tier the visual importance they need as anchor-figures in the vertical rows. In the figure of virgin no. 6, minute details such as the geometric patterns on the border of her cloak, on the cords and the jeweled tassels of her sash, on the architectural elements of the baldachin, and even on the seams of her pointed shoes, all attest to the preservation of good twelfth-century carving beneath the shiny coating of mastic. The fluent folds falling from her left hip and the lines of the sash suffer minor distortions from the inset above her knees. Nevertheless, the drapery of the left hip, thigh, and lower leg provides close comparisons with the drapery defining the right hip and thigh of tympanum angel no. III, and the lower legs of angels nos. II and V (Plate IIc–d).

The drapery of Foolish Virgin no. 7 appears to be too coated and worn to have much interest or to provide valid comparisons. Even so, the general original arrangement still pertains in the upper half of the figure, and from the waist down some ornamental details survive on the cords and tassels of the knotted belt. The loop of drapery in her left hand seems to be a separate cloth or scarf similar to those held by virgins nos. 1, 3, and 8 and is not part of the other draperies of her garments.

Those scarves raise an iconographical question about the accuracy of the restorations of the virgins' heads. Although Guilhermy said that none of the vestiges of the original sculpture made any distinction between the apparel of the Wise and Foolish Virgins, he may have been mistaken.[14] The heads of Wise Virgins nos. 1 and 2 have veils, and traces of the original veil survive on the right shoulder of virgin no. 3. Unfortunately recutting destroyed all evidence for Wise Virgin no. 5, and no. 4 has no remnants of original hair or veiling. Across the doorway, the twelfth-century hair of Foolish Virgin no. 6 establishes her original unveiled state. The unrecut twelfth-century hair of virgin no. 10 extends up to the level of her right ear and also lacks any vestige of a covering veil. In the figures of the other two Foolish Virgins, no remnants of head coverings survive. The two marvelous twists of hair that cross the breast of virgin no. 9 and extend to mid-thigh prove the most distinctive aspect of the figure. Although not conclusive, the combined evidence in no way contradicts the medieval customs or conventions that are attributable to the recommendations and urgings of Tertullian, an early Church Father, concerning the proper headdress for Christian women. To connote their status, he recommended that maidens leave their heads uncovered and that married women wear veils. Although not closely adhered to before the twelfth century and often ignored then, his recommendations became rigid custom from the thirteenth until the sixteenth century.[15] The surviving evidence in the jambs raises the possibility that those customs were honored in the figures of the virgins. A representation of the Foolish Virgins as maidens without veils would have been iconographically correct and would have differentiated them from the veiled Wise Virgins who, when "the bridegroom came . . . went in with him to the marriage" (Matthew 25:10).

Although general recutting pervades the surfaces of the drapery of Foolish Virgin no. 9 and ranges from heavy to light, her remarkable twists of hair survived untouched, and the area that they frame also proved to be free of reworking, except for the surface of the lamp. Nevertheless the shape of the lamp, a repetition of those held by virgins nos. 4, 6, and 8, seems to have the correct twelfth-century profile. The architectural surround also shows evidence of light recutting. Unfortunately the ensemble as a whole has been stripped of its original character.

The final figure on the right jamb, Atlantid no. 6a, allows two important comparisons that underscore the close stylistic relationship of the entire ensemble to the work of the Master of the Tympanum Angels. The insets and recutting in no way altered the basic and unusual arrangement of the drapery festooning his figure. The seemingly unique and idiosyncratic arrangement (except for the parody achieved by the restoration of figure no. 1a) has a counterpart in the scarves of the tympanum angels (see especially nos. II, III, and IV, Plate IIc–d). Moreover, although they are heavily coated, the concentric incised folds of the swag that covers his loins seem to replicate the lap drapery of the figure of Abraham (Fig. 24).

89

The unity of style of the sculpture of the jambs, of the inner archivolt, and of the upper tympanum angels creates a corpus of work from the hand of a most versatile artist, who is consistent in his attitude toward the human body, in his ability to make forms exist in three-dimensional space, and in the fluency of his line. Of the vast repertoire of drapery conventions, the Master of the Tympanum Angels had a distinct preference for a number of them, which he used with imagination and which have helped to establish his style. He gave the iconographically integrated sculptures of the jambs, lintel, first archivolt, and the center section of archivolts II, III, and IV a formal unity as well. Specific details, his stylistic trademarks, occur throughout this carefully ordered and well-planned ensemble. His artistic ideas emerge even in the small figures of the Resurrected Dead and in the surviving fragments of the scenes of the Damned. Although the hand of the Master of the Tympanum Angels does not appear in the figures of the patriarchs, even there he obviously had an influence.

THE JAMB COLONNETTES

On both sides of the portal, richly ornamented colonnettes stand in the angled recesses of the jambs. The shafts of the colonnettes in place today are copies, "moulées sur pierre factice" (molded of manufactured stone), taken from the original shafts now in the Musée de Cluny in Paris (Plates Xa and XIa).[16] To illustrate his eighteenth-century study of the signs of the zodiac carved in the Paris region, Le Gentil de la Galaisière published prerevolutionary drawings indicating that the designs on the pair of shafts molded and now used for all three portals originally adorned only the right sides of the north and south portals.[17] Unfortunately no such drawings exist for the central portal, but a recently discovered small fragment in the Musée Municipal de Saint-Denis contains designs that do not appear in either of Le Gentil's drawings (Fig. 27). The continuous vine on the fragment follows a vertical course, unlike the encircling spirals on the shafts pictured by Le Gentil and on their copies now in situ. The disposition of the rinceau and the little nude armed with a lance and shield resembles the combatants intertwined in a vertical vine on a fragment of a colonnette from Saint-Denis now in the reserve of the Musée de Cluny (inv. 11659a). The other face of the fragment has pairs of confronted birds. The tails of each pair terminate in a palmette that forms the support for a small nude

THE JAMB SCULPTURES

FIG. 27. Fragment of the shaft of a recessed colonnette from the right jamb, central portal. Musée Municipal de la Ville de Saint-Denis

figure. The eighteenth-century engraving showing only that face of the shaft with the confronted birds testifies to the original location of the fragment on the left jamb of the right, or south, portal.[18] The monsters on the adjacent face of the fragment in the Musée Municipal, although upside down, closely resemble the confronted and adorsed monsters and birds on the Cluny fragment. The

91

lithe, active, and well-articulated bodies of the combatants on the adjoining face of each colonnette are also strikingly similar. Le Gentil's drawing did not show this face of the Cluny colonnette, which indicates that it was positioned so that one would see the combatants only on entering the church by the right portal.[19]

The two fragments—one in the Cluny, the other in the Musée Municipal—with the vertical rinceau and similar nude combatants must have been carved by the same artist. The thick trunks of the vines, their tendrils similarly disposed, link the two, as does the increased modeling of the forms compared with that of the two colonnettes now in situ. But taken as a whole, the decoration on all the colonnettes reflects the same taste for "surornementation," or decoration that covers the entire surface. Characteristically, the highlights of the surfaces contrast with shadows of the negative spaces created by cutting back from the surface plane, and those shadows activate the overall designs. That preference for "surornementation" also governed the decorated surfaces of the Apostle bas-relief discovered at Saint-Denis during the excavations of 1947.[20] It emerges again at Chartres in the decoration of the intercolonnettes between the statue-columns, and in other early Gothic doorways, especially at Le Mans and Bourges.[21] At Saint-Denis the small nudes that twist and turn in the tendrils of the vines reflect the same interest in human anatomy demonstrated by the sculptor of the Resurrection frieze in the lintel zone of the central tympanum.

As diagrammed, the bases of the jamb colonnettes consist of nineteenth-century insets (Plates Xb and XIb). In the lateral portals the bases, although recut and badly worn, retain designs identical to those pictured in the Le Gentil drawings. The lively figures, animal and bird as well as human, forming the bases raise the possibility that similar figures also occurred on the originals in the central portal.

The capitals surmounting the jamb colonnettes of the central portal survive from the twelfth century, although their unequal size and dissimilar design might cause one to think otherwise. On the left side, the joining of two horizontal masonry beds bisects the capital between its two tiers of stylized acanthus leaves. On the right jamb, the smaller, apparently truncated capital, also lacking a decorated abacus, may reflect adjustments similar to those affecting the virgins, their niches, and their baldachins.

Two long, rectangular panels decorated with stylized foliage in palmette designs fill the spaces above the capitals of the colonnettes. The designs, quite consistent with the other ornament of the portal, show evidence of superficial recutting. The masonry joints that divide them into three parts conform to the regular twelfth-century beds 29.5 cm. high. Because Suger mentioned a lintel on which he had his famous petition inscribed, the symmetry of the panels on opposite sides of the portal has given weight to the argument that in the twelfth century, the tympanum rested on a lintel scaled to the overall height of the panels and supported by the trumeau with a statue-column representing St. Denis.[22] To perform its function, any lintel would have to span the doorway and rest on the jambs. Trisected by the joints of three beds of twelfth-century masonry, the panels present a structural arrangement incompatible with the hypothesis supposing an adjacent lintel commensurate with the heights of the panels. Then too, the continuous plain borders that frame the foliate panels would have separated them from any such lintel. Thus, the self-containment of the framed panels also seems at variance with the hypothesis.

In addition, the eighteenth-century drawing by Martellange (Fig. 2) shows the trumeau rising directly to the tympanum without an intervening lintel of any consequence. But if, in fact, the original design had included a substantial decorated lintel, then like the missing portions of the baldachins above the uppermost virgins on the jambs (nos. 4 and 9), the initial intention may have been sacrificed to expediency at the time that the portal was assembled. Like the one in place today, a narrow lintel above the foliate panels would have had formal as well as structural validity. The proportions of the panels and of the foliate designs, vertically organized and bold in scale, appear inconsistent with the visual demands of the hypothetical lintel. The panels seem designed to continue the supportive function implicit in the Atlantids and recessed colonnettes that decorate the jambs on the same axis. The sum of those parts would have constituted a design with the formal sophistication that characterizes the overall composition of the sculptural ensemble. The evidence strongly refutes the hypothesis that originally the portal included a lintel similar to those at Moissac and Beaulieu. In sum, all inconsistencies now apparent in the design may have their explanation in terms of the unforeseen adjustments to accommodate the great twelfth-century bronze doors.

THE DECORATED PLINTHS AND BASES

Although the stated limits of this study preclude discussion of the lost statue-columns of the central portal (Fig. 1),[23] brief mention of the decorated plinths, bases, capitals, and abaci of the embrasures is necessary in order to supplement the diagrams of the jambs (Plates Xb and XIb). Carved under the direction of Debret, the eight decorated columns that replaced the statue-columns obviously date from the nineteenth century (Plate I).[24]

Decorated plinths above a flattened continuous torus serve as visual connectors between the decorated portions of the portal and the plain surfaces of the mural masonry that extend below today's pavement down to the foundations. The carved ornament in regular panels of lightly incised designs creates an uninterrupted horizontal band of ornament extending from the flanking buttresses across the embrasures and jambs (Plates Xa and XIa). Rather than one continuous design, each block supporting a column presents its own vegetal or geometric pattern. The original joint of the horizontal masonry beds lies in the upper narrow scotia between the torus and the plinth. As elsewhere, interruptions in or a lack of such a mortared joint betray the nineteenth-century insets, which are identified in the diagrams. Identical patterns originally decorated both faces of each projecting block. Deviations from the norm also disclosed the presence of a nineteenth-century masonry repair, as, for example, on the left jamb, in the first plinth to the left of Wise Virgin no. 1 (Plate Xb). On the assumption that the plinths presented almost the only original designs of the portal decoration still in situ, Stoddard analyzed the ornament in detail.[25] He described the designs as "almost draftsmanship with stone as a medium," which accurately emphasizes the contrast of that decoration, originally about eye level, with the more deeply articulated relief of the ornament in the upper portions.

The same masonry bed containing the blocks of stone forming the plinths also includes the bases of the columns. That zone of the embrasures presents a number of interesting, if still unresolved, problems. An obvious formal distinction exists between the profiles of the twelfth-century bases of the nineteenth-century columns (bases composed of a torus, filet, slanting scotia, filet, and flattened torus) and the vestiges of the adjacent, continuous decorated molding, nearly columnar in profile, which, despite severe mutilations and recutting, still functions visually as a "base" for the undulating surfaces between

FIG. 28. Base, plinth (restored), and intercolumnar molding on right side of portal, detail of fourth embrasure

the columns (Fig. 28). Similar continuous moldings survive in better condition in the right embrasures of the right portal. Almost unretouched, that parallel arrangement authenticates the remains of the molding on the central portal as part of the original decoration.

Above that molding the twelfth-century masonry surfaces, although badly eroded and often replaced or recut, show no traces of any carved ornament. Proposals that the intercolumnar surfaces originally had decoration, as at Chartres, seem untenable.[26] Evidently those continuous curving or undulating surfaces that simulate attached colonnettes provided adequate articulation in the eyes of the twelfth-century master responsible for the central portal.

As diagrammed (Plates Xb and XIb), the twelfth-century bases supporting the nineteenth-century columns are either recut or restored with nineteenth-century insets. The bottom tori of some of the bases and the adjacent continuous molding retain curious anatomical remnants carved into their surfaces:

Left side: second embrasure, a foot;
              third embrasure, an arm with the hand grasping a heel;
              base of fourth column, a foot (Fig. 28).
Right side: base of first column, the tip of a ratlike tail.

Any attempt to associate those vestiges with the figurate consoles beneath the feet of the statue-columns pictured in the Montfaucon drawings (Fig. 1) falters because the evidence proves too fragmentary to support conjectures.[27]

FIG. 29a. Abacus frieze of twelfth-century heads in rinceau formed by the arched wings of doves, below third and fourth archivolts, left

FIG. 29b. Abacus frieze with twelfth-century head in foliate rinceau, below second archivolt, right

THE CAPITALS AND ABACI

The capitals and abaci from which the archivolts spring create continuous friezes of ornament across the top of the embrasures (Figs. 29a–b and Plate I). Both survive in better condition than the sculptures in the lower portions of the portal. Only the first capital in the right embrasure, next to Foolish Virgin no. 9, underwent noticeable recutting. Its foliate palmette design with a clasp binding the elements together recurs frequently in the vocabulary of Dionysian ornament. The design of each capital, enhancing the visual unity of this band of ornament, continues across the entire masonry block. The blocks extend horizontally beyond the capitals to create the equivalent of a capital above the adjacent intercolumnar surface. And finally they penetrate the masonry behind the next capital in the stepped embrasure. The unbroken or continuous torus of the astragal provides an additional horizontal linkage, emphasizing the artistic intent to create a continuous frieze of ornament.

Each capital, or block, has a different design, which injects variety into the visual continuum.[28] Composed in an identical manner, the capitals of the clustered piers in the western bays within the portals provide another early example of the continuous capital—a concept conspicuous in Gothic sculptural decoration and distinct from the double capitals of Romanesque buildings.[29] With one exception, the designs on the capitals of the central portal typify the early Gothic development of stylized foliate patterns, often grouped symmetrically into several zones. The exception, the second capital in the left embrasure, presents adorsed, birdlike bodies with human heads turned toward each other. Part of an ornamental palmette design, those figures perpetuate Romanesque principles. Although slightly retouched, their heads and feathered bodies add to the corpus of surviving twelfth-century carving on the portal. An interesting variant on the arrangement of the stylized acanthus leaf occurs on the fourth capital in the left embrasure. Small projecting leaves with curled, drooping tips form four horizontal rows around the core of the capital (Fig. 29a). An unusual design, it also occurs among the pier capitals in the western bays and in the foliate ornament of the crypt.

The abacus frieze above the capitals provides a continuous horizontal accent even more prominent than that created by the astragals below the capitals. The scale, rhythmic flow, and deep undercutting of the abacus designs add to their visual impact. On the left side of the portal the frieze has a sequence of stylized birds whose arching, outstretched wings join to create an undulating line that encloses a series of small, slightly grotesque faces capped by leaves forming inverted palmettes (Fig. 29a). Except for recutting on the south face above the first column, the frieze appears untouched by the restorer. Across the surfaces of the four abaci on the right side of the portal, tendrils curve back from a vine with leaves that enfold or cup small heads. Although corroded and worn, the heads appear characteristic of the Dionysian facial style (Fig. 29b). The stem of the vine is continuous except for interruptions as it rounds some of the corners—another detail adding to the accumulating evidence that the entire sculptural ensemble was carved in the workshop, not in situ, and assembled on completion. Here on the right, or south side of the portal, as usual, the stone erosion is less severe than on the north side, and recutting above the jamb is lighter and more sporadic. The striated hair, beards, and mustaches, and the faces with bulging eyes provide examples in miniature of the facial style of Suger's workshops.[30]

THE OLD TESTAMENT PATRIARCHS, OR ELDERS OF THE APOCALYPSE, ON THE THREE OUTER ARCHIVOLTS

Above the embrasures on the left and right, in the three outer archivolts, the twenty-four elders of the Apocalypse sit in orderly tiers "round about the throne" (Apocalypse 4:4). According to the vision of the Second Coming revealed to John of Patmos, they carry musical instruments and vials filled with "odours which are the prayers of saints" (Apocalypse 5:8). As mentioned in Chapter 4, the figures in the fourth and outermost archivolt occupy niches formed by an intertwined vine iconographically equated with the Tree of Jesse. Its presence here refers to the descendants of Jesse as the ancestors of the crucified Christ of the tympanum. The Tree of Jesse symbolically unites the patriarchs of the Old Testament with the elders of the Apocalypse.[1] (The imagery of the Tree had not previously appeared in monumental sculpture.) The choice of the epithet "Master of the Elders" follows the usual identification of the twenty-four figures, but giving them the label "patriarchs" acknowledges the significance that the conflated identities bring to overall interpretation of the sculptural ensemble.

The nineteenth-century restorations to the figures replaced all twenty-four heads with the usual unfortunate visual result. Three twelfth-century heads identified as coming from Saint-Denis and now in the collection of the Louvre belonged to three of the patriarchs or elders in the archivolts (Figs. 13a and 30a–b). Proportionally compatible with those figures, the Louvre heads have measurements that also accord with the mean measurement of the nineteenth-century replacements.[2] But once again, instead of the monumental, abstract style of the twelfth-century heads, the nineteenth-century faces provide bland, devitalized imitations. In trying to reproduce the large, bulging twelfth-century eyes rimmed with flat ridges or bands, the restorer created blank, sightless ones devoid of the awesome intensity of the prototypes. The smooth contours and

FIG. 30a.   Twelfth-century head originally belonging to patriarch Y, fourth archivolt, right, fourth tier. Paris, Musée du Louvre, cat. no. 55

FIG. 30b.   Twelfth-century head originally belonging to patriarch O, third archivolt, right, first tier. Paris, Musée du Louvre, cat. no. 52

FIG. 30c.   Detail of patriarch O, third archivolt, right, first tier, with plaster cast of head. Paris, Musée du Louvre, cat. no. 52

planes of the moon-faced nineteenth-century heads capture nothing of the stark-
ness of the original three. Quite primitive in feeling, two of the three surviving
faces are elongated to the point of distortion. The third, somewhat broader
through the eyes, appears more normally proportioned.

The restoration took even greater liberties with the headdresses. Nothing
about the mutilated headcoverings of the twelfth-century survivors suggests
precedents for the various bonnets, cloches, toques, and hats, both hard and
soft, that the patriarchs now wear. The vestiges of the original headdresses,
although shaved and cut back, sit like crowns, quite low and nearly horizontally
on the patriarchs' brows. Traces of beading and jewels also survive on the headdress of Louvre head cat. no. 52. The combined evidence, although not conclusive, favors the identification of those vestiges as crowns—attributes conforming to the biblical description: "And round about the throne were four and
twenty seats; and upon the seats four and twenty ancients sitting, clothed in
white garments, and on their heads were crowns of gold" (Apocalypse 4:4).[3]

In addition to the three heads in the Louvre, which may have been in place
when the restoration began, vestiges of the original hair and beards survived to
guide the restorer. As the diagrams show, remnants of beards greatly out-
number traces of hair (Plates VIb, VIIb, VIIIb, and IXb). Beard ends, short and
long, usually divided, sometimes crimped or twisted, remain in sixteen of the
twenty-four figures. A comparison of the fragments visible on the collars
and chests of patriarchs C, D, G, P, and T show the remarkable variety possible
in the arrangement of those terminal locks alone. The windblown beard of patriarch C seems especially noteworthy (Plate VIa). A gust of wind from the
northwest seems to have lifted one of the twelfth-century locks and flattened
it against the right stem of the enframing vine. In restoring the head, the
nineteenth-century sculptor perpetuated that original conceit.

Patriarch C and four others in the fourth archivolt, patriarchs F, J, M, and
Z, suffered extensively from the combined effects of exposure, iconoclasts,
and restoration. The severe recutting that accompanied inept insets distorted
the anatomy in the lower portions of patriarchs F and J. Yet those two, unlike
patriarch C, at least retain their basic twelfth-century poses and drapery
arrangements (Plate VIa).[4] Of the two demi-figures within the topmost niches
of the Tree of Jesse (patriarchs M and Z; Plate Va), only the foliage that terminates the enframing vines retains enough of the unspoiled carving to have value
and interest today. Although showing mutilations and losses, the curling

100

fronds as they close in upon themselves or occasionally shelter a stylized bud or cluster of small fruits typify the lively handling of Dionysian foliate forms. At times fully undercut, the leaves and stems create a lacework pattern reflecting a general and marked increase in the depth of undercutting. Once again, as the distance from the viewer increased, so did the forward projection and under-cutting of the sculptures. In the archivolts, as elsewhere, the sophistication of composition and of formal organization equals that of the iconography.

Although patriarchs M and Z have not always been accepted as part of the original arrangement, enough of the old stone survives to certify that the demi-figures perpetuate the original plan, even to the position of the heads which, on the right in the bust of patriarch Z, conforms to the requirements of the surviving twelfth-century hair on his shoulder.[5] By placing those two small busts in the uppermost niches of the vine rather than making full-length, seated figures, the twelfth-century artist again showed his formal sophistication. As well as accommodating to space limitations, he also avoided overwhelming the archivolts with an arrangement visually too heavy or weighty for that upper, central location.

Although badly weathered, recut, and repaired, the other five figures of the fourth archivolt, patriarchs L, P, S, V, and Y, generally retain the original drapery arrangements and much of their twelfth-century character. Neverthe-less, as diagrammed, each one has a particularly disfigured area, which must be noted and avoided whenever those draperies are cited for comparisons or used as examples of the development of artistic ideas (Plates VIIb, VIIIb, and IXb).

In the second and third archivolts, the condition of the figures varies from the nearly perfect figure of patriarch T (Fig. 32 and Plate IX) to the almost completely recut drapery of patriarch R and the deformed lower portions of patriarch H, cited in Chapter 2 as an example of the most drastic recutting (Plates VIIb, VIIIb, and IXb). Patriarchs B, E, R, and W also belong on the list of heavily restored figures in the middle two archivolts, although each retains at least one area of particular interest that will receive attention. For instance, before extensive recutting and skinning, patriarch W, the uppermost figure in the third archivolt, right, probably would have ranked among the best sculp-tures in the middle two archivolts and numbered among the most skillfully carved figures in terms of interesting variations on mid-twelfth-century drap-ery conventions. In particular, the well-preserved drapery over the lower legs and the unretouched foliate console on which his feet rest give evidence of the

101

quality and fluency of the original carving (Fig. 33). The richly ornamented borders of the tunic collar, left sleeve, and hem contrast with the relative simplicity of the other elders' garments. As the diagrams indicate, recutting, more than any other aspect of the restoration, has deprived this group of the vitality of the original carving. By and large, the twelfth-century arrangements of the draperies survive, but often the restorer's chisel has so blurred the folds composing the familiar twelfth-century drapery conventions that, in the aggregate, the draperies have lost much of their clarity as well as their vigor.

The remaining figures in the second and third archivolts, patriarchs A, D, G, K, N, O, Q, T, and U, survived the restorations better than the figures already discussed. Although the diagrams pinpoint many recut areas as well as a variety of small, scattered insets, especially in figures A, K, O, Q, and U, those patriarchs remain valuable examples of the twelfth-century work. For instance, the recutting proved so light in the lower drapery of patriarch A that the figure is able to provide the key to the identification of the work of the sculptor whose ideas dominate the carving in the archivolts (Fig. 31).

The characteristics of this artist's hand seem quite distinct from those that distinguish the Master of the Tympanum Angels and the Master of the Apostles, although all three used many of the same drapery conventions and, without doubt, interacted in their deliberate efforts to create a harmonious ensemble. Nevertheless, since the sculpture reflects their differences, detailed analyses of several figures in the archivolts are needed to reveal enough stylistic idiosyncracies to identify the dominant hand in the archivolts, the artist who merits the title Master of the Elders.[6]

The upper half of the figure of patriarch A survives in excellent condition, whereas the lower half shows only the lightest recutting. In fact, the mortar filling the eroded joints proved the most disfiguring aspect of the restoration. As the diagram indicates (Plate VIb), the figure also required several small insets, among them the blunt, square, bare feet flanking the restored central palmette of the foliate footrest. His nineteenth-century feet and toes compare unfavorably with the slender, anatomically correct feet of patriarch N on the opposite side of the portal (Plate VIIIb), whose feet survive from the twelfth century and give credence to the restoration of patriarch A as barefooted.

Since only two of the twenty-four patriarchs are barefooted, those exceptions present an iconographical enigma. By the mid-twelfth century the Deity,

FIG. 31. Patriarch A, second archivolt, left, first tier

Christ, the Apostles, and angels were conventionally represented with bare feet, and the Virgin, patriarchs, prophets, elders, and other biblical and holy personages were shod. Moissac is one of the notable and somewhat earlier exceptions where all of the elders are depicted barefooted. Several biblical references to bare feet may have inspired those of the two patriarchs at Saint-Denis. In the Old Testament, bare feet were associated with a holy place and with sorrow and weeping. The first biblical reference occurs in the Lord's injunction to Moses: "Put off the shoes from thy feet, for the place whereon thou standest is holy ground" (Exodus 3:5). Another occurs in a similar injunction to Joshua; as a

103

result of those texts, removing shoes became an act of reverence, so that priests customarily went barefooted while officiating in the temple (Josue 5:16). Such an interpretation would accord with the symbolism here: the barefooted patriarchs flanking the entrance to the church would make a specific reference to holy ground, the church, which is equated with the Heavenly City and with the New Jerusalem of the Apocalypse (Apocalypse 21:1–3, 10–14).

The reference to sorrow seems no less appropriate to the bare feet of the two figures who flank the scene conflating the Crucifixion with the Second Coming. One of the two Old Testament references associating bare feet with sorrow involves David at the time of Absalom's conspiracy. David "went up by the ascent of Mount Olivet, going up and weeping, walking barefoot, and with his head covered" (2 Samuel 15:30). That Old Testament association seems especially pertinent if the harp-playing, barefooted patriarch A should be identified as King David. The biblical gloss by the Venerable Bede provides a plausible identification for the other barefooted figure, patriarch N. Bede, referring to the ancestors of Christ in the genealogy of the Book of Matthew (1:1–17), equated David and Abraham with two columns that stand in front of the door which is Christ.[7] The metaphor of the columns derives from the two columns before the door to the Temple of Solomon, in itself a symbol of the church (3 Kings 7:15, 21).[8] Authenticated as twelfth-century iconographical details, doubtless the bare feet and the harp playing were intended to add new layers of meaning to the patriarchal ensemble.

Patriarch A is short, with squat proportions in comparison to the adjacent elders on his right and the two above him. Accommodation to the expanding arcs of the archivolts necessitated figures of differing heights. Although most of the seated patriarchs occupy five voussoirs, patriarchs G, O, and Q actually extend across six. On the left side of the portal, none of the figures in the archivolt covers six voussoirs, but the necessary expansion was achieved by the use of several outsized voussoirs. Patriarch A in the lowest tier is carved in less pronounced relief than the upper figures, as is true throughout in the lower levels of the portal. The shallower projection increases the impression of compact proportions. The form and volume of his anatomy, although neither unsubstantial nor exaggerated, seem somewhat subordinate to the richly patterned design of the drapery.

The elongated torsos of patriarchs G and O, their narrow, sloping shoulders, and the exceptionally stiff, narrow pleating of the drapery cascades that fairly bristle along the hem edges raise the question again of stylistic variations attributable to an assistant. Although the same narrow shoulders and fine, bristling pleats recur in the elongated torso of patriarch B, the outsized figure of patriarch Q has the stocky proportions more typical of the Elder Master's style. Because such variations are infrequent (or, as in the proportions of the fourth archivolt figures, reflect limitations imposed by the enframing vines), and because the distinctions lie for the most part within the framework of the master's artistic ideas, the sculpture deserves to be considered as an ensemble that expresses his style. Attempts to isolate areas of a figure attributable to an assistant would be a pedantic as well as an extremely dubious exercise.

Typical of all of the elders, the costume of patriarch A consists of two simple garments, an ankle-length tunic under a light mantle or cloak. In over half of the figures, the drapery of the mantle also covers the lap and continues in an arrangement, often quite complicated, over the knees and lower legs. *Galons*, broad jeweled or ornamental collars, band the necks of the tunics, but, as noted, only patriarch W has a decorated hem (Fig. 33). One other figure, patriarch B, has a patterned border edging his mantle, and in four instances the sleeves of the tunics have ornamented cuffs (patriarchs A, O, Q, and W). Such details commonly embellish the garments of other figures on the portal, but in general, the costumes of the elders appear less lavish than those of the Apostles.

Since the musical instruments and vials carried by the elders cover large areas of the upper drapery, the most distinctive elements of the Elder Master's style occur in the lower portions of the seated figures and in the sleeves and drapery over the shoulders. As the mantles fall lightly over the tunics, the arrangement of their folds and the overlapped cascades of drapery afforded the artist his greatest opportunity to create interesting patterns. Formed by a thin, often seemingly brittle material, the mantles define the anatomy they cover, but at the same time assume independent and often arbitrary surface designs. The usual tensions resulted from the artist's discrepant use of natural folds and stylized conventions. In his most arbitrary arrangements, he frequently confused the folds of the tunic with the overlapping mantle, and he often failed to make a clear distinction between the fabric of the mantle and that of the sleeve.

The well-preserved drapery of patriarch A exemplifies those confusions in the visually striking, multipleated fall of material from the left wrist and in the contrived cascade of pleated foldbacks beside the right leg (Fig. 31). The latter demonstrates the artist's preoccupation with the complication of a design. In the combination of materials from the mantle and tunic, the component parts become quite indistinguishable, especially along the intricate, convoluted, and overlapped hem. In the unnaturally stiff diagonal fall of drapery from the left arm, the zigzag of foldbacks falling from the wrist merge arbitrarily with those of the lower portions of the mantle and finally with the tunic undergarment. A notable variant on that complex pattern occurs in the intricate drapery of patriarch T, particularly along his left side (Fig. 32).

The treatment of the short overlap on the left knee of patriarch A also distinguishes the hand of the Master of the Elders from his companions. Sharp fluted ridges separate rhythmic hollows that respond to the projecting, rounded form of the knee. The mortar that repaired the masonry there caused some distortion to the drapery, but similar, more complicated, and better-preserved examples cover the knees of patriarchs K and T. The same type of fluted drapery recurs in the arrangements veiling the hands of patriarchs F, J, L, and T. Along the hem, the splayed inner edges of the symmetrical underfolds typify this master's treatment of that much-used convention, in contrast with the closed form favored for the central foldbacks by the Master of the Tympanum Angels. Although the Angel Master never employed the fluted arrangement covering the knees, its use by the Apostle Master provides telling comparisons. On the left knee of Apostle no. 31 (Plate IVa), similar drapery with softer and flatter ridges and fluting defies gravity to follow and accent the diagonal line of the shank. Less crisply executed, that more arbitrary arrangement also has rounded, thicker hem edges evoking heavy materials associated with the Apostle Master. They contrast in texture with the brittle, thin edges that characterize so much of the drapery of the Master of the Elders.

In the stylized folds of the zigzag cascades and in the overlapped fold on the right thigh, the artist depicted the mantle of patriarch A as a light, flexible textile. He expressed the same texture even more explicitly in the thin line of the hem of the mantle that forms a diagonal across the legs of patriarch U, and in the similar but somewhat recut hemlines slanting across the legs of patriarchs D, E, and Q. The thin, lightly defined drapery over the legs of patriarch A contrasts with the heavy, curving folds that sag below his left forearm and with the firmly incised tubular folds defining his upper arm. That seemingly illogical variation in the quality of the fabric forming parts of the same garment illustrates the artist's primary concern for variety in the surface patterns of the drap-

FIG. 32. Patriarch T, second
archivolt, right, third tier

ery. Nevertheless, the patterns neither obscure nor distort the natural definition
of arms and legs that are essentially normal in their proportions.

The varied details of the drapery of the twenty-four elders exhibit another
recurrent convention that helps to identify the work of this master. In keeping
with his ingeniously overlapping folds and contrived patterns, he occasionally

FIG. 33.   Detail of hemline and console of patriarch W, third archivolt, right, fourth tier

used a purely decorative swirl, or gathering, along the hemline of the tunic. Such a device occurs in the drapery between the ankles of patriarch A, where a gathering of small folds seems to emerge through a slit, or opening, in the border of the tunic. In the hemline beside the ankle of patriarch T, an even more contrived flourish occurs where the swag of folds crossing the shank meets the vertical fall of pleats beside the leg (Fig. 32). Less pronounced but related stylizations embellish the lower borders or hems of patriarchs R and W (Fig. 33).

Despite many shared conventions, the Master of the Elders treated the hemlines of the tunics quite differently from those carved by the Master of the Tympanum Angels or by the Apostle Master. A certain stiffness infects even the most fluid of the hemlines in the archivolt figures (see patriarchs A, N, T, V, and W). His most severe treatment of a hem seems especially rigid and brittle when compared with the curving, sinuous lines created by the hems of the

FIG. 34.   Foliate console supporting feet of patriarch D, second archivolt, left, second tier

Apostles' tunics or by those of the Wise and Foolish Virgins on the jambs (see especially patriarchs G, O, Q, and U; virgin no. 8, Fig. 26; and Apostles, Plates IIIa and IVa). In addition, the manner in which the Elder Master depicted the inner or back hemline differed from the handling of the same convention by the other two masters. The deeply undercut front hems of the patriarchs' tunics and their prominent feet subordinate the back hems. Despite full artic- ulation, the contours of those hemlines are modified by shadow in the recesses above the foliate consoles, especially those of patriarchs D, K, and Q. In contrast, the Apostle Master used the inner hemlines as a background for the feet and as a well-defined frame that helped to organize the figures into groups. Frequently the Master of the Elders also depicted the inner surfaces and back edges of folded leaves on the consoles in a manner echoing the convention of the inner hemline (see, for example, those of patriarchs A, D, N, Q, T, and W, Figs. 31–33).

109

All the foliate consoles below the feet of the elders of the middle two archivolts deserve close attention as an important part of the sculpture in the archivolts. Their rhythmic designs, balanced but never rigidly symmetrical, display the technical skills of the master both in the articulation of the foliate forms and in the depth of undercutting (Figs. 33 and 34). In almost every instance, the placement of the elders' feet proves integral to the balance and to the pattern. Infinitely varied, the designs include vegetal forms such as the out-of-scale acorn and cluster of berries in the console below patriarch A (Fig. 31), and the somewhat mutilated bud on a stem projecting on central axis in the palmette below patriarch T (Fig. 32). In the latter design, the boldly conceived foliage emerges from the clasp, or circular band, that holds the bases of the leaves together—a typical Dionysian conceit. As noted in Chapter 5, the deep undercutting and centrally organized designs of the footrests contrast with the lower relief and overall patterns of the foliate consoles below the scenes of Paradise and the Elect in the first archivolt (Plates VIa and VIIa).

Although tensions exist between natural and arbitrary forms in the figures of the patriarchs, the master consistently demonstrated his knowledge of anatomy. In his depiction of hands that hold the attributes and play the musical instruments, his observation of bone structure seems especially keen and sensitive. An unexpectedly large number of the hands have survived untouched by the restorer except for minor repairs or minimal recutting. Their comparison with other original hands both in the Apostle frieze and in the figures of the Wise and Foolish Virgins of the jambs further distinguishes the style of the Master of the Elders (Figs. 9, 15a, 25a, and 26). Despite the nineteenth-century insets in the index and middle fingers of the right hand of patriarch A, the unusually elongated fingers demonstrate the artist's knowledge of and interest in the process of plucking and stopping the strings of a harp.[9] With even more elaboration he modeled the well-preserved and bony fingers of patriarchs Q and R (Plate VIIIa). Other hands with a high degree of naturalism conforming to the type survive in the figures of patriarchs B, D, G, K, N, O, T, W, and Y. Although delicacy and sensitivity also characterize hands carved by the Apostle Master, with the single exception already noted of Apostle no. 32, their more rounded, softer forms distinguish them from the work of the Master of the Elders. Only the right hand of Apostle no. 32 approaches the structural precision and sinuous elongation of the patriarchs' hands, and that exception seems to demonstrate the artists' influence on each other. Despite their elongation, the patriarchs' hands never show the disproportion that typifies many of the hands of the Wise and Foolish Virgins attributed to the Master of the Tympanum Angels.

The vials held by all but two of the elders also reflect the artist's interest in accurate imagery. The vase carried by patriarch B—a well-preserved example with only the lightest recutting on its rounded bowl and none at all on the long neck encircled with jeweled bands—closely resembles the famous royal *justa* (ceremonial vase) given by Louis VII to Suger, who eventually presented it to the patron saints of the abbey.[10] The similarities in form and decoration seem more than coincidental and suggest that the artist deliberately chose the royal gift as his model.

The musical instruments reveal the same meticulous attention to detail.[11] The artist accurately carved tightly twisted wire strings that coil from right to left around the tuning pegs along the upper frames of the harps held by patriarchs A and N (Fig. 31 and Plate VIIIa). Carved with even more precision, the instrument held by patriarch R has similar twisted wires, but only for the longer bass strings; single, untwisted strands represent the strings in the higher range. Other well-observed details, such as the bow of patriarch D and the finial on the harp of patriarch H, testify to the fidelity of the artist's observations of twelfth-century instruments (Plates VIa and VIIa). The small animal-head finial still has its carefully articulated ears and eyes, as well as incised caricaturing lines on the face. Presumably the worn animal-head finials of the harps held by patriarchs E and R once had similar details (Plates VIa and VIIIa).

Although the wealth of well-preserved detail made the figure of patriarch A an excellent example of the Elder Master's style, patriarchs K, N, and T, despite variations in posture, degree of relief, and drapery arrangements, also belong within the scope of this versatile artist, and each adds to the definition of his style.

In the figure of patriarch N, the artist exuberantly restated and elaborated the ideas discussed in the analysis of patriarch A.[12] But patriarchs K and T, in the upper reaches of the archivolts, present significant developments within the master's style (Fig. 32 and Plate VIIa). The edge of the mantle falling from the right shoulder of patriarch K reaches almost to his left knee where, forming a graceful swag, it loops over the left wrist. The increased relief and surface

111

modeling and the greater depth of undercutting that distinguish this detail have counterparts in the drapery of patriarch T. The unusual plasticity of the stylized gathering beside the elder's left ankle, the deep undercutting of the folded-back edges in the cascade of drapery falling from his left wrist, and the strong modeling of the insistent parallel folds that suggest overall pleating endow the stylizations in the drapery of patriarch T with an unexpected plausibility and naturalism. In effect, the increased modeling that compensated for the increased distances of those figures from the viewer also resolved the tensions of contrasting ideas that are so apparent in the lower figures, and which are especially pronounced in the drapery of patriarch A. As well as increasing the surface modeling, the artist also achieved a greater sense of volume through increasing the projection of the figures from the surface plane. The vase, the veiled right hand, and the vielle resting on the left knee of patriarch T have such a realistic forward projection and visual prominence that they dominate the entire figure.

Although somewhat modified by mortar repairs along the eroded masonry joint and by sporadic light recutting, the folds overlapping the knees of patriarch K belong in the same category as the ridged and fluted drapery covering the left knee of patriarch A. Involving both the left and right knees, patriarch K's arrangement resulted in a more complicated design incorporating a series of deep V-shaped folds across the lap. In conception and handling the series closely resembles not only the perfectly preserved V-shaped folds between the knees of patriarch T, but also the drapery defining the lap of the central figure of Christ in the tympanum. In all three arrangements, the deep incisions between the diagonal ridges produce heavy shadows that underscore the active surface patterns.

A survey of artistic ideas that dominate the figures of the patriarchs would be incomplete without citing what survives of particular interest in the figures of patriarchs D, G, O, and U. Patriarch U ranks among the most competent achievements of the Master of the Elders (Plates VIa, VIIa, VIIIa, and IXa). Although his pose is contorted to a degree that has no equal among the elders, his figure nevertheless shows no distortions. Prominent diagonals still emphasize the reversed positions of the upper and lower portions of the elder's body, despite the recutting that occurred along the smooth surfaces of his left and right thighs. The easy, natural folds of the end of the mantle rest lightly on the seat of the bench and provide an unexpected note of reality juxtaposed with the strongly incised, insistent fold defining the oval of his right thigh. Although now distorted by recutting, the drapery defining the right leg of patriarch H (Plate VIIb) probably originally paralleled that of patriarch U. In pose and degree of surface modeling, the two figures on opposite sides of the portal appear to balance each other. Despite fairly pervasive but not distorting recutting, the neighboring figures of patriarchs L and Y, the uppermost full figures in the fourth archivolt, still give evidence of pronounced modeling and surface plasticity typical of the best-preserved drapery in the upper reaches of the archivolts.

With the exception of the new head, minor recutting, and a few small insets along the masonry joints, as diagrammed, patriarch G remains essentially intact (Plate VIIb). In contrast to patriarch A, the torso of the figure appears considerably elongated, and his shanks seem unconvincingly foreshortened—relative proportions already noted as being somewhat dependent on the additional voussoir required for adjustment to the expanding arc of the second archivolt. The complicated cascade of overlapping drapery that falls from his right shoulder to his ankle exaggerates the elongation. In conception, the cascade has an equivalent in the fall of pleats along the left side of patriarch T, but the flat, stiff rendering of patriarch G's cascade has an even closer affinity with the bristling falls of drapery from the right shoulder and beside the left leg of patriarch O—another figure with elongated proportions also attributable in part to the expansion of the arcs in each successive archivolt (Plate VIII).

The restorations caused some distortion in the figure of patriarch O, as well as a confusion in the drapery falling from his left shoulder. The recutting that pared the silhouette of that shoulder and upper arm also completely eliminated the seat of his bench below. The mantle, originally responding to the contours of the seat, curved over it realistically. Now no longer supported by the bench, the arrangement could be mistaken for a gravity-defying stylization. Considerable recutting of the area above the left knee reduced the foreshortened ridge of the thigh, thereby creating another distortion that accentuates the elongation of the torso. Except for occasional recutting, as diagrammed, the rest of the figure retains its original appearance. The twisted torso and crossed arms and feet enliven and give variety to the seated figure, and the elaborate drapery seems designed to emphasize the complicated pose.

113

FIG. 35. Detail, Tree of Jesse showing typical simplification of forms as vine crosses voussoir joints, fourth archivolt, right, at junction of sixth and seventh voussoirs

The lower portion of the figure of patriarch D (Plate VI) provides yet another well-preserved example of the quality and style of the Master of the Elders. Almost as well preserved as the flaring pleats along the hem, the deeply undercut foliage of the footrest typifies the intricacies of Dionysian variations on the basic palmette design (Fig. 34). Viewed in the aggregate, the consoles show considerable variation in scale and boldness of the foliate designs. Both in the scale of the leaves and the degree of projection, the consoles of patriarchs D and W (Plate IXa) rank with the bolder arrangements.

The visual prominence and scale of the foliage is usually repeated on the opposite side of the portal in the footrest of the patriarch occupying the equivalent location. That balance contributes to the sense of order in the overall composition. The distribution of musical instruments also reveals the artist's same concern with the composition—a concern shared by the other artists at Saint-Denis. Eight of the twelve pairs of elders occupying parallel locations on opposite sides of the portal carry identical instruments (Plate I). The order underlying the schema shows a subtle alternation of those pairs, with additional variations in the placement of the instruments. Reflecting a preference for balance without absolute symmetry, that order, intuitively understood by the viewer, is best revealed in a diagram.[13]

Other subtle variations in the arrangement of the elders implement the artist's conception not only of order, but also of rhythm. Even the disturbing visual effect of the assorted headdresses invented by the restorer does not destroy the deliberate variations in the scale of the figures within an archivolt—again variations with equivalents on the opposite side of the portal. The rhythmic patterns depend not only on scale and on the numerical progression of figures represented in the second, third, and fourth archivolts, but also on variations in poses and in richness of surface designs.[14]

With the exception of the Deity in the keystone of the third archivolt, every archivolt figure occupies two or more voussoirs. Three of the patriarchs spread across as many as six stones. Despite the difficulties that several stones per figure present to the sculptor in the workshop, careful examination produced no evidence suggesting that the voussoirs were carved in situ—a procedure that would have been contrary to customary practice. Evidence accumulated during the examination of the jambs and embrasures tends to confirm that carving was done in the workshop. The masonry system, the type of stone used, and numerous structural discrepancies discussed earlier indicated that the decoration below the level of the archivolts was carved in the workshop and then assembled and inserted into the masonry of the facade.[15] Above the level of the jambs, the scant evidence available also points to the final assemblage and insertion of completed sculpture with, at most, only minor adjustments made in situ to accommodate the carving on either side of a joint. For instance, the overall view of the archivolts shows masonry joints directly above and below each patriarch (Plate I). The divisions between figures and groups of figures appear to have been designed both to facilitate carving in units and to minimize problems in final assemblage. Contrived so that only stems and trunks meet at the joining of two voussoirs, the vines of the fourth archivolt have no delicately carved and undercut foliate forms overlapping the masonry joints. On the right the junction of the outer vine, where the sixth and seventh voussoirs abut, provides a revealing example of how easily the forms could be merged at a joint (Fig. 35). The trunk of the vine of the sixth archivolt fused readily with the fully

115

articulated stem in the seventh. The minimal need for accommodation of the lower portion to the upper one at the masonry joint simplified the task of the sculptor during installation, when he had to work from scaffolding.

Another detail suggests that the two large tympanum stones were not in place at the time they were carved. The design of the foliate molding framing the hemicycle varies somewhat in the upper and lower stones (Plates IIc–d, IIIa, and IVa). The two versions of the continuous, vertically organized palmette frieze probably reflect, as already proposed, that one hand was responsible for the zone containing the seated Apostles and another for the tympanum angels of the upper stone. In effect, the two foliate designs prove so harmonious that the differences, like those of the figure styles, do not startle the viewer but emerge only on close examination.

A third hand also worked on the sculpture of the tympanum. The figure of Christ, which spreads across both the upper and lower stones, seems closely affiliated stylistically with the figures of the Master of the Elders. Although the differences in scale complicate comparisons, the attitudes of the artist and the ideas expressed in the figure of Christ have the greatest consonance with the figures of patriarchs K and T (Fig. 32 and Plates I and VIIa). As noted earlier, the concentric V-shaped folds between their knees provide remarkably close comparisons. In general, their draperies reveal the same preoccupation with surface pattern in all three figures, and pronounced modeling invigorates comparable series of highly stylized conventions that combine to create the overall drapery designs. The hand of the Master of the Elders seems equally apparent in the deep undercutting of the hem, in the large scale of the prominent feet, and in the crisp and fully undercut edges of the mantle and of its overlapped cascades as well as in the splayed inner edges of the symmetrical underfolds. Although seriously affected by the fracture cutting diagonally across the left side of the figure, the arrangement of drapery over Christ's left leg develops into a swirl typical of this master. Both in form and in the handling, it is comparable with the drapery across and beside the left leg of patriarch T. The careful articulation of the skeletal structure of Christ's torso seems an extension of the artistry and precision with which the Master of the Elders rendered the bony, elongated hands of the patriarchs. The torso of Christ contrasts with the softer forms of the bodies in the Resurrection frieze and inner archivolts—the work of the Master of the Tympanum Angels, who emphasized the musculature of the torso rather than its bone structure. Before the nineteenth-century recutting under the right armpit and along the ribs—a repair that deprived the upper portion of Christ's body of the original, substantial volume—the proportions of the figure would have approximated those of the seated figures of the patriarchs. Christ's proportions contrast sharply not only with the stumpy figure of Abraham, the only seated figure associated with the Angel Master, but also with the generally short-waisted figures of the seated Apostles. The same volume noted in the analysis of the figure of patriarch A also exists beneath the active surface patterns of Christ's drapery.[16]

CHAPTER 8

STYLE AND MEANING
IN THE CENTRAL PORTAL

In establishing stylistic relationships among the figures of the central portal, one becomes particularly conscious of three distinct artistic statements. Because virtually all of the original heads are missing, identification of the work of different artists depended on the proportions of the figures and on the distinguishing characteristics of their drapery, hands, and feet. Although the foregoing detailed comparisons emphasized their differences, the sculptors did not work independently of each other. Throughout the portal, certain common ideas prevailed that deserve the label "Dionysian characteristics," that is, characteristics attributable to art of the premier abbey church dedicated to St. Denis.

First and perhaps foremost, all three artists shared an interest in natural forms—an interest that gave rise to a number of Dionysian features. The delicately carved feet of the Apostles, the elongated, bony hands of the patriarchs, the softer, subtly modeled bodies in the Resurrection frieze, and the stark anatomical explicitness of Christ's torso all show the new concern for naturalism. Characteristically, the artists created solid, unsubtle forms beneath the drapery. Each artist varied the poses and drapery arrangements of the figures and, where possible, the placement and conformation of the attributes, thereby endowing each figure with distinctive aspects—a concept reflecting the new humanism, which attached dignity and value to the individual.

The artists eschewed the frenzied agitation associated with Romanesque figures and their draperies. Variety in pose was invariably achieved without sacrificing the sense of the figures' composure. A new calm pervades the Saint-Denis portal figures. Their gestures, without exception, all seem credible and restrained. The new preoccupation with verisimilitude not only reduced distortion to a minimum, it also increased the artists' interest in creating volumes that existed in space. An increase in forward projection and in surface modeling and the overlapping of forms implemented their new ideas. Breaking away from the Romanesque respect for the surface plane of the stone, all three artists carved figures that project from the planes rather than lie behind them. Yet in varying degrees, the tension between natural forms and stylizations characterized the work of all three. Nevertheless, the subtle increase in the projection of the figures within a group as the distance from the viewer increased— a major factor in the overall composition of the portal sculpture—had the ultimate effect of reducing those tensions.

Although many of the artistic ideas associated with the Romanesque aesthetic were discarded in the portal, Romanesque conventions persisted. The artists constantly drew on the vast storehouse of Romanesque drapery conventions, but each used them in a distinctive way that helped to define his particular style. The Languedocian fold, the tubular fold, the incised hook fold, and circular folds that accent an anatomical entity or pinpoint a joint occur throughout the sculptural ensemble. The inner or back hemline depicted drooping below the front hem and behind the feet, a less common convention, emerges as a typical Dionysian feature that constantly recurs in the work of all three artists. The detailed analysis that isolated each artist's style also traced the interaction and exchange of artistic ideas among them that helped to make their sculpture visually compatible. But the intimate cooperation, especially in the tympanum sculpture, was possible primarily because the artists were implementing a detailed and completely integrated plan. Certainly the unity of the plan with its ordering of the zones represents an aspect of the portal that should be rated as a major Dionysian contribution. That clarity of composition, its balance and order, contrasts with the agitation, the horror vacui, and the resulting excitement of Romanesque portals.

Balance emerged as a fundamental concept of design in the building campaigns sponsored by Abbot Suger. The architectural principle used in planning the western bays into which this portal gives entrance depended on the concept of a mirror image (identical but reversed forms on either side of an axis), and that principle also regulated the plan of Suger's choir.[1] The master masons, responsible ultimately for the decoration as well as the construction of the new building, quite obviously accepted the principle of balance as fundamental for the creation of a harmonious whole. In obeying it, the sculptors avoided static monotony by constant variation within their constituent units.

In its sophistication, the formal organization equaled that of the iconographical program of the portal, and each depended on the other. The iconography gained clarity from the composition, which, in turn, benefited from the interrelationship and complexities of the ideas represented. For instance, the zones of the tympanum resulted in a didactic clarity quite unknown in Romanesque representations of the Last Judgment. The ordering of the tympanum into prescribed zones in which figures form a frieze is reminiscent of the schema of the Christian universe and of the Last Judgment found in the sixth-century *Christian Topography* by the Alexandrian Cosmas Indicopleustes.[2] The division of tympana into zones became a characteristic carried even further in High Gothic portals.

In the archivolts, the intertwined vine of the Tree of Jesse forms a niche for each of the fourth archivolt figures and also provides a frame for the entire sculptural ensemble above the jambs. The vine, which equates the elders of the Apocalypse with the patriarchs and ancestors of Christ, the major figure on the central axis, frames a representation that selectively refers to the entire history of the Christian universe as understood by medieval theologians. The sculptural program encompasses that version of world history, spanning events from the Fall of man, a reference implicit in the angel with the flaming sword set by the Creator to bar the way to the Tree of Life, through the continuum represented by the Old Testament precursors of the crucified Christ, and finally to the raising of the dead by the angel sounding the last trumpet, the Second Coming of Christ, and Last Judgment. The visual focus and the theological and intellectual emphasis reside in the representations on the central axis in both the tympanum and archivolts. In addition, stylistic unity links the iconographically united subjects of the jambs, lintel zone, and first archivolt. The Master of the Tympanum Angels was responsible for that carefully interrelated ensemble, as well as for the Trinity and censing angels of the center archivolts.[3]

In the carefully composed ensemble, the intention to interconnect figures and ideas emerges in another important Dionysian detail. The upper Wise and Foolish Virgins located in the lintel zone turn their attention toward the adjacent scenes of Heaven and Hell. Their respective focuses, one on the Heavenly City and the other on the scenes of Hell, make the visual and iconographical interrelationship of the sculptures on the jambs, lintel, and inner archivolt quite specific. The subtler interrelationships within a group, particularly in the Apostle zone, were achieved through formal devices of considerable sophistication. Yet that concern with composition gave rise to some arbitrary stylizations, such as the device of the back hemline used to band together a group of figures. Inevitably, tensions between the individual and the group arose with the new emphasis on the integrity of each figure which, at the same time, had to conform to the requirements of the artistic plan.

Although the Dionysian concern for naturalism disallowed the Romanesque treatment of figures as patterns, minor lapses remind the viewer of that discarded aesthetic. The tensions between natural and stylized forms seemed greatest within single figures. The original heads, powerful and abstract (Figs. 13a, 14, and 30a–b), must have contrasted strikingly with the delicate and sensitive rendering of the hands of the patriarchs. Ideas filtered through the prism of three distinct artistic intelligences bring to the fore the international character of Suger's workshops. Although Suger stated that he "convoked the most experienced artists from diverse parts," he mentioned only one region, Lorraine, noted for the metalwork of the goldsmiths.[4] Scholars have sought to identify other regional influences suggested by the various stylistic expressions visible in the portal sculpture. Sauerländer observed that "a variety of styles formed the sculptures on the west doorways," but concluded that "it is no longer possible to reach definite conclusions." He then added, "The predominating models seem to have come from Toulouse and its sphere of influence."[5] In the central portal alone, we have observed how three artists shared in experimenting with new concepts and forms that resulted in an explosion of artistic ideas within a figure, with results not necessarily compatible but always interesting.[6]

In summary, the sculpture of the late 1130s at Saint-Denis provides a laboratory in which one can observe the filtering of artistic ideas through the sensibilities of artists of different backgrounds. Although the sculpture of the central portal looks to the future in its synthesis of new formal and aesthetic ideas, the backgrounds, training, and ingrained predilections of those artists account for the persistence of *retardataire* elements and Romanesque traditions and conventions. The respect for the integrity of human proportions—a reflection of the dawning humanism—and other innovative concepts such as iconographical and compositional unity, spatial depth, and corrections for optical perspective fertilized those earlier traditions and sparked stylistic mutations that introduced the Gothic style.

As its first significant by-product, the detailed study of the nineteenth-century restorations of the central portal of Saint-Denis has identified areas of unspoiled twelfth-century carving of exceptional quality. Those revelations have allowed the distillation of the basic elements of each artist's style, as well as the recognition of the characteristics common to all three. The precise information accumulated and presented here now allows valid comparisons with other twelfth-century sculpture and the identification of both the genealogy and the legacy of the artistic and iconographical ideas generated in the Saint-Denis workshops assembled by Suger.

In an impassioned diatribe against the restorations at Saint-Denis, that "Panthéon de la monarchie" and the first Gothic edifice, Didron asserted: "Il n'y a pas un profil, pas une sculpture, pas un parement dans toute la surface du monument qui n'aient été raclés, modifiés, arrangés. Personne . . . n'est capable de discerner . . . dans Saint-Denis l'ancien du moderne, pour conserver l'un et remplacer l'autre."[7] The documentation by the diagrams of every aspect of the restorations to the central portal indicates the legitimate basis for the anguished protest; at the same time the diagrams themselves refute Didron's pessimistic conclusion published nearly a hundred and fifty years ago.

PLATES

LEGEND

JAMB SCULPTURES

1–5	Wise Virgins
1a	Atlantid
6–10	Foolish Virgins
6a	Atlantid

TYMPANUM

Frieze of the Resurrected Dead

11a–c	sarcophagus with coquettish woman
12a–c	three figures
13a–c	three figures
14	sarcophagus with Suger kneeling
15	figure
16a–b	sarcophagus with bishop or king
17a–b	two figures
18a–b	sarcophagus with contorted figure and mutilated figure
19a–c	sarcophagus with hair-pulling figure

Apostle frieze

20	trumpeting angel
21–26	Apostles
27	Virgin Mary
28–33	Apostles
34	angel with flaming sword
I	Christ
II–V	angels carrying symbols of Passion

ARCHIVOLTS

VI	Gate to Paradise with Blessed
VII	Archangel "Gabriel"
VIII	Abraham with souls
IX	angel presenting soul
X	Judging Christ
XI	angel presenting soul
XII–XV	Damned
XVI–XVII	censing angels
XVIII	Deity with Lamb
XIX	Dove with angels
A–Z (except I and X)	patriarchs/elders of the Apocalypse

Schema to identify the location of the sculptures of the central portal (F. Bland, del.)

KEY TO DIAGRAMS

19th-century insets

recut surfaces of 12th-century stone

repairs of fractures and joints with mortar, mastic, cement, gesso

unrepaired fractures postdating 19th-century restoration

PLATE I

CENTRAL PORTAL

PLATE IIa

TYMPANUM, CENTRAL PORTAL

PLATE IIc

TYMPANUM ANGELS, NOS. II AND III, LEFT

PLATE IId

TYMPANUM ANGELS, NOS. IV AND V, RIGHT

PLATE IIIa

TYMPANUM, LEFT, MIDDLE AND LOWER ZONES

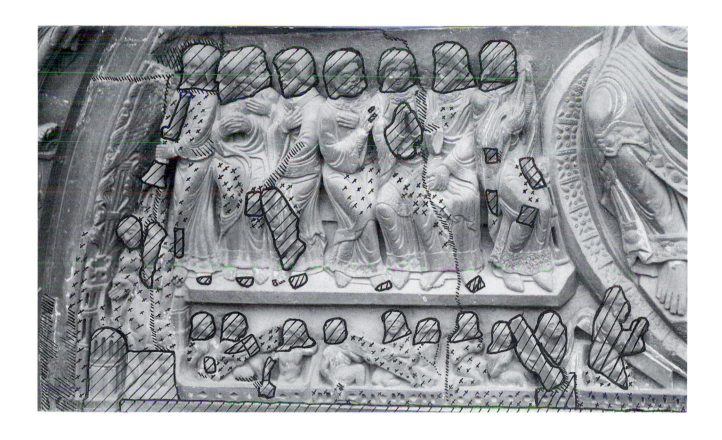

DIAGRAM OF RESTORATIONS TO
FIGURES NOS. 5, 11–14, AND 20–27

DIAGRAM OF RESTORATIONS TO
FIGURES NOS. 10, 15–19, AND 28–34

PLATE Va

ARCHIVOLTS, CENTER

DIAGRAM OF RESTORATIONS TO FIGURES NOS. IX–XI,
XVI–XIX AND PATRIARCHS K, W, M, AND Z

PLATE VIa

ARCHIVOLTS, LEFT, FIRST TWO TIERS

PLATE VIb

DIAGRAM OF RESTORATIONS TO FIGURES NOS. VI AND VII
AND PATRIARCHS A–F

ARCHIVOLTS, LEFT, UPPER TIERS

PLATE VIIIa

ARCHIVOLTS, RIGHT, FIRST AND SECOND TIERS

PLATE VIIIb

DIAGRAM OF RESTORATIONS TO FIGURES NOS. 10, XIV,
AND XV AND PATRIARCHS N–S

PLATE IXA

ARCHIVOLTS, RIGHT, UPPER TIERS

DIAGRAM OF RESTORATIONS TO FIGURES NOS. XI–XIII
AND PATRIARCHS T, U, W, Y, AND Z

PLATE Xa

WISE VIRGINS, LEFT JAMB

DIAGRAM OF RESTORATIONS TO WISE VIRGINS NOS. 1–4

PLATE XIa

FOOLISH VIRGINS, RIGHT JAMB

DIAGRAM OF RESTORATIONS TO FOOLISH VIRGINS NOS. 6–9

SHORT TITLES
AND ABBREVIATIONS

The following short titles and abbreviations are used throughout the notes.

Bmon   *Bulletin monumental*

Crosby (1987)   Crosby, Sumner McKnight. *The Royal Abbey of Saint-Denis from Its Beginnings to the Death of Suger, 475–1151.* Edited and completed by Pamela Z. Blum. New Haven, Conn., 1987.

Crosby et al., *Saint-Denis*   Crosby, Sumner McKnight, Jane Hayward, Charles Little, and William Wixom, eds. *The Royal Abbey of Saint-Denis in the Time of Abbot Suger (1122–1151).* New York, 1981.

Gautier, ms. 11681   Gautier, Ferdinand-Albert. "Journal qui fait suite à Félibien." Paris, Bibliothèque Nationale, nouv. acq. ms. fr. 11681.

Gerson, ed., *Abbot Suger*   Gerson, Paula Lieber, ed. *Abbot Suger and Saint-Denis. A Symposium.* New York, 1986.

Gerson, *West Facade*   Gerson, Paula Lieber. *The West Facade of St.-Denis. An Iconographic Study.* Ph.D. diss., Columbia University, New York, 1970. Ann Arbor, Mich. (UMI, 1970, no. 73-26, 428).

Guilhermy, ms. 6121   Guilhermy, Ferdinand François, baron de. "28 Notes historiques descriptives sur l'abbaye & basilique de St Denis." Paris, Bibliothèque Nationale, nouv. acq. ms. fr. 6121. [This manuscript has both page and folio numbers. It is cited here by page numbers.]

J.W.C.I.   *Journal of the Warburg and Courtauld Institutes*

Panofsky, ed., *Suger*   Panofsky, Erwin, ed. and trans. *Abbot Suger. On the Abbey Church of St.-Denis and Its Art Treasures.* Princeton, N.J., 1946. 2nd edition: Gerda Panofsky-Soergel, ed. Princeton, N.J., 1979.

P.L.   Migne, Jacques-Paul, ed. *Patrologia latina cursus completus . . . Series latina,* Paris, 1844–64.

Suger, *De administratione*   Suger. *Liber de rebus in administratione sua gestis.* In Panofsky, ed., *Suger,* 40–81.

Suger, *De consecratione*   Suger. *Libellus alter de consecratione ecclesiae Sancti Dionysii.* In Panofsky, ed., *Suger,* 82–121.

NOTES

CHAPTER 1

1. On the architectural prototypes in the Ile-de-France for the chevet at Saint-Denis, see Jean Bony, *French Gothic Architecture of the Twelfth and Thirteenth Centuries* (Berkeley and Los Angeles, 1983), 22–43, 49–60; idem, "What Possible Sources for the Chevet of Saint-Denis?" in Gerson, ed., *Abbot Suger*, 131–42; and Stephen Gardner, "L'Eglise Saint-Julien de Marolles-en-Brie et ses rapports avec l'architecture parisienne de la génération de Saint-Denis," *Bmon* 144/1 (1986): 7–31.

2. The designation "Romanesque" was restated recently for the portals of Saint-Denis and Chartres in a volume of the Zodiaque series presenting Romanesque sculpture by region: Anne Prache, *Ile-de-France romane,* La Nuit des temps 60 (1983), 71–82. For the author, the west facade of Saint-Denis carried the germ or seed of the future, but too much of the Romanesque tradition tied it to the past. Because Prache found no clear definition of the style to come, she stated that the portals proper could not be defined as Gothic. See also Millard Fillmore Hearn, *Romanesque Sculpture: The Revival of Monumental Stone Sculpture in the Eleventh and Twelfth Centuries* (Ithaca, N.Y., 1981), 191–215, where the west portals of Saint-Denis and Chartres and the Sainte-Anne portal of Notre-Dame de Paris are all included in a group described as the second generation of great Romanesque portals.

3. Henri Focillon, *Art of the West,* 1, *Romanesque Art,* ed. Jean Bony (Greenwich, Conn., 1965), 105.

4. Sumner McKnight Crosby, "The Creative Environment," *Ventures,* Magazine of the Yale Graduate School (Fall 1965): 10–15; and idem, "An International Workshop in the Twelfth Century," *Cahiers d'histoire mondiale* 10 (1966): 19–30.

5. On the regency and for a summary of Suger's career, see Eric Bournazel, "Suger and the Capetians," in Gerson, ed., *Abbot Suger,* 55–72; Panofsky, ed., *Suger,* 1–37; and Crosby (1987), 85–101.

6. Suger, *De administratione,* in Panofsky, ed., *Suger,* 40–41. Panofsky reproduced and translated part 2 of *De administratione* as well as the complete texts of Suger's two other works concerned with his abbacy and patronage of the building campaigns: *Libellus alter de consecratione ecclesiae Sancti Dionysii,* in ibid., 82–121; and *Ordinatio A.D. MCXL vel MCXLI confirmata,* in ibid., 122–37. Suger wrote of his part in

administering the abbey's affairs in the first twenty-three chapters of *De adminis-tratione,* published by Auguste Lecoy de la Marche, ed., *Oeuvres complètes de Suger recueillies, annotées et publiées d'après les manuscrits pour la Société de l'Histoire de France* (Paris, 1867), 155–85. See also Giles Constable, "Suger's Monastic Administration," in Gerson, ed., *Abbot Suger,* 17–32.

7. Suger, *De administratione,* in Panofsky, ed., *Suger,* 50–53, 86–89. The Merovingian church had been constructed under the patronage of King Dagobert I and lavishly embellished through his generosity. The legend of Christ's consecration endowed the nave with a special sanctity. Suger and his contemporaries also mistakenly reckoned Dagobert as founder of the abbey. Excavations in this century have shown that Dagobert's patronage actually involved only the enlargement of the church of circa 475, then extant. For the archaeological evidence for the earlier structures, see below, nn. 24, 25, 27, 28.

8. Suger, *De consecratione,* in Panofsky, ed., *Suger,* 86–89.

9. Ibid., 88–89.

10. Suger, *De administratione,* in Panofsky, ed., *Suger,* 46–47.

11. Crosby's excavations uncovered the foundations of a twelfth-century nave and transepts begun in Suger's time but never completed: Crosby (1987), 267–77, 339–52. On the architecture of the eastern extension, see, inter alia, William W. Clark, "Suger's Church at Saint-Denis: The State of Research," in Gerson, ed., *Abbot Suger,* 105–130; Crosby (1987), 215–65; and above, n. 1.

   The upper stories of Suger's choir were rebuilt in the thirteenth century in a campaign that also replaced the Carolingian nave with the one that exists today in the French rayonnant style of the 1230s: Caroline Astrid Bruzelius, *The Thirteenth Century at Saint-Denis* (New Haven, Conn., 1985).

12. For the extent and documentation of Suger's travels, see Otto Cartellieri, *Abt Suger von Saint-Denis, 1081–1151* (Berlin, 1898).

13. "Magistrorum multorum de diversis nationibus": Suger, *De administratione,* in Panofsky, ed., *Suger,* 72–75. See also ibid., 42–43, 46–47, 58–59.

14. Ibid., 48–49. Suger also wrote about the gilded bronze doors he ordered for the central portal and recorded the verses inscribed thereon; ibid., 47–49.

15. On the program of the north portal and the possible subject of the lost mosaic, see Pamela Z. Blum, "The Lateral Portals of the West Facade of Saint-Denis: Archaeological and Iconographical Considerations," in Gerson, ed., *Abbot Suger,* 218–27.

16. Suger, *De administratione,* in Panofsky, ed., *Suger,* 64–65.

17. Ibid., 48–49.

18. Ibid., 62–65.

19. In essence, the Pseudo-Areopagite postulated an ordered universe with hierarchical substrata forming an endless chain of being. All had been brought into being by the Trinity, the primal source or superessential Godhead, whom the Pseudo-Areopagite equated with Light. But all strove to return to, to know, and to become one again with that Light: Dionysius the Pseudo-Areopagite, *The Ecclesiastical*

Hierarchy, ed. and trans. Thomas L. Campbell, Ph.D. diss., Catholic University of America, 1955 (Washington, D.C., 1981); and idem, *Oeuvres complètes du Pseudo-Denys, l'aréopagite,* ed. and trans. Maurice de Gandillac (Paris, 1943). See also, inter alia, Panofsky, ed., *Suger,* 18–25; Grover A. Zinn, Jr., "Suger, Theology, and the Pseudo-Dionysian Tradition," in Gerson, ed., *Abbot Suger,* 33–40; Paula L. Gerson, "Suger as Iconographer: The Central Portal of the West Facade of Saint-Denis," in ibid., 183–98; and Blum, "Lateral Portals," 215–18, in ibid.

20. Hilduinus abbas s. Dionysii, *Areopagitica sive Sancti Dionysii vita, P.L.* 106, cols. 13–24. For the literature and a summary of the development of the triple identity of the patron saint, see Crosby (1987), 4–5, 453–55 nn. 5–17.

21. Abelard, having found refuge at Saint-Denis after his castration, questioned the identification of St. Denis with Paul's convert Dionysius the Areopagite. Abelard's exposé of the improbable conflation of identities was based on the writings of Bede. It so angered Abbot Adam that he accused Abelard of treason and forced him from the abbey. Soon after, when Suger became abbot, he dropped the charge but imposed the condition that Abelard never enter another monastery: Panofsky, ed., *Suger,* 17–18.

22. For the literature and a summary of the development of the legend, see Crosby (1987), 5, 455–56 nn. 18–25.

23. [Fortunatus], *Passio sanctorum martyrum Dionysii, Rustici et Eleutherii* [known also as the *Gloriosae*], in *Monumenta Germaniae historica,* ed. Bruno Krusch, Auct. antiq. 4, pt. 2 (Berlin, 1885), 101–105.

24. Crosby (1987), 15–17, postulated that those huge Gallo-Roman masonry blocks decorated with *peltae,* or *boucliers d'Amazones* (Amazons' shields), had been reused in the foundations of the church built on the site in circa 475. On the basis of information and dating of the sarcophagi provided him by other archaeologists excavating early burials on the site, Crosby also concluded that St. Denis had been buried in a previously existing cemetery.

25. An article proposes that the Gallo-Roman masonry blocks should be dated to the late third or early fourth century, and that they were not Gallo-Roman *spolia,* reused in the church of circa 475, but part of the first structure erected above the saint's grave in his honor about fifty years after his martyrdom: Patrick Perin, "Quelques considérations sur la basilique de Saint-Denis et sa nécropole à l'époque mérovingienne," in J.-M. Duvosquel and A. Dierkens, eds., *Villes et campagnes au moyen âge: Mélanges Georges Despy* (Liège, 1991), 599–624. Perin's hypothesis rests on a dating earlier than previously supposed for some of the sarcophagi, which by their location had to be associated with the mural masonry containing the huge decorated Gallo-Roman blocks. The new dating would modify some of Crosby's conclusions that were based on the old dating: see above, n. 24.

26. *Vita Genovefae virginis Parisiensis,* in *Monumenta Germaniae historica,* ed. Bruno Krusch and Ernst Dümmler, Script. rer. Mer. 3 (Hanover, 1896), 204–38.

27. On the 475 church, see Crosby (1987), 13–26 and plan, pl. 3.

28. See ibid., 29–50 and plan, pl. 3.

29. Suger, *De administratione,* in Panofsky, ed., *Suger,* 70–71.

30. Ibid., 42–43. As an act of penance for the sins of his father, Charles Martel (ca. 690–741), Pepin left orders that he be buried face down before the threshold of the basilica: ibid., 44–45. On the Carolingian church, see Crosby (1987), 51–83 and plan, pl. 3 verso.

31. Suger, *De administratione,* in Panofsky, ed., *Suger,* 42–45.

32. In the earliest surviving royal charter, dated 625 and signed by Clothaire II, St. Denis is described as Clothaire's particular patron: "sancti domini Dioni[nsis p]eculiares p[atroni] n[ostri]": Philippe Lauer and Charles Samaran, *Les Diplômes originaux des Mérovingiennes. Facsimilés phototypiques avec notices et transcriptions* (Paris, 1908), 4 and pl. I.

33. On the events that occurred at the tomb and the miracles ascribed to St. Denis, see Crosby (1987), 8.

34. On the abbey as the royal pantheon, see ibid., 9–12.

35. Although the royal regalia were kept at Saint-Denis, Reims cathedral had been the place of coronation from the time of Clovis I. For the history of the abbey as the repository, see ibid., 10–11.

36. For the siege and pillaging of Saint-Denis in 1435, see Michel Félibien, *Histoire de l'abbaye royale de Saint-Denis en France* (Paris, 1706), 347–48; and for that of 1567, ibid., 398, and also Dom F. Jacques Doublet, *Histoire de l'abbaye de S. Denys en France* (Paris, 1625), 1313–14, 1347–49. For a reference to the pillaging and occupation of the abbey again in 1591, see Sumner McKnight Crosby, *The Abbey of St. Denis 475–1122,* 1 (New Haven, Conn., 1942), 6; and for a summary of events affecting the abbey from the fourteenth to the late eighteenth century, idem, *L'Abbaye royale de Saint-Denis* (Paris, 1953), 66–70.

37. Gautier, ms. 11681, published in part in *Le Cabinet historique* 20/1 (1874): 280–303; 21/1 (1875): 36–53, 118–35; and by H. Herluisson and P. Leroy, "Le Manuscrit de Ferdinand-Albert Gautier, organiste de l'abbaye de Saint-Denis," *Ministère de l'instruction publique et des beaux-arts,* Reunion des Sociétés des Beaux-Arts et des départments 29 (1905), 236–49.

38. Gautier, ms. 11681, 20. Some of the sculpture from Saint-Denis was sold in 1774, when the Marquis de Migieu acquired one of the statue-columns from the cloister (now in the Metropolitan Museum of Art, New York) for his château at Sauvigny-les-Beaune. See, inter alia, Pierre Quarré, "L'Abbé Lebeuf et l'interprétation du portail de Saint-Bénigne de Dijon," in *Actes du Congrès Lebeuf* (Auxerre, 1960): 3; and on the statue as coming from the cloister at Saint-Denis, see Vera K. Ostoia, "A Statue from Saint-Denis," *The Metropolitan Museum of Art Bulletin,* n.s. 13 (June 1955): 298–304. See also Léon Pressouyre, "Did Suger Build the Cloister at Saint-Denis?" in Gerson, ed., *Abbot Suger,* 236–38.

39. François Debret, "Réponse aux observations critiques . . . adressée à Monsieur le Ministre des Travaux publics au sujet des travaux de restauration exécutés à l'église

royale de St Denis," Seine, Saint-Denis, Dossier de l'Administration 1841–1876, Paris, Archives de la Commission des Monuments historiques, fol. 19 (hereafter, Debret, "Réponse"). The order to destroy the statues directed that they be treated as sacred objects, thereby indicating that the monks believed them to represent saints or holy persons.

40. For the original drawings, see Montfaucon, "Desseins et gravures pour la monarchie françoise," Paris, Bib. Nat., ms. fr. 15634, vol. 1, fols. 33–77, reproduced by Bernard de Montfaucon, *Les Monumens de la monarchie françoise,* 1 (Paris, 1729), pls. XVI–XVIII.

41. For earlier iconographical interpretations of the statue-columns, see J. Vanuxem, "The Theories of Mabillon and Montfaucon on French Sculpture of the Twelfth Century," *J.W.C.I.* 20 (1957): 45–58; and Gerson, *West Facade,* 14–49. Gerson postulated that the statue-columns were an integral part of each portal program and the means of unifying and amplifying the iconographical meaning within each one: ibid., 149–58. For application of that theory in an interpretation of the left portal program, see Blum, "Lateral Portals," 209–18, in Gerson, ed., *Abbot Suger.*

42. Guilhermy, ms. 6121, p. 59. He later summarized the notes in an unsigned article: "Saint-Denis: Restauration de l'église royale," *Annales archéologiques* 1 (1844): 400–411.

Guilhermy, ms. 6121, p. 233, also wrote that Legrand d'Aussy had stated from his own experience that the engravings of Montfaucon did not in the least resemble the originals, that poses had been changed, accessories and emblems eliminated, draperies modified, and heads altered. Guilhermy based that assertion on a passage he had misinterpreted in Pierre-Jean-Baptiste Legrand d'Aussy, *Des Sepultures nationales, et particulièrement de celles des rois de France . . .* (Paris, 1824), 268–69. Legrand d'Aussy was referring not to the statue-columns but to tomb effigies still extant that had been sent to the Musée des Monuments français and were later returned to the abbey.

For a list of objects from Saint-Denis on display, see, inter alia, Alexandre Lenoir, *Description historique et chronologique de sculpture réunis au Musée des Monumens français* (Paris, an VIII de la République [1800]), 3–6, 125, 142–45, 149, 156–60, 162–64, 165–66, 167–69, 170, 171–73, 174, 175, 184, 186, 188, 198–200, 204–205, 210–11.

43. For heads of three kings, see Marvin C. Ross, "Monumental Sculptures from Saint-Denis: An Identification of Fragments from the Portal," *The Journal of the Walters Art Gallery* 3 (1940): 90–109, including an appendix by Rutherford J. Gettens, "Note on the Microscopic and Chemical Examination of Specimens of Stone from Sculptured Stone Heads," 108–109. For the head of a queen, see Léon Pressouyre, "Une Tête de reine du portail central de Saint-Denis," in *Essays in Honor of Sumner McKnight Crosby,* ed. Pamela Z. Blum, *Gesta* 15 (1976): 151–60; also Crosby et al., *Saint-Denis,* 39–43, cat. no. 3. For the most recent discovery of another head of a king acquired by the Musée de Cluny, see Fabienne Joubert, "Tête de Moïse provenant

du portail de droite de l'Abbatiale de Saint-Denis," *Revue du Louvre* 38 (1988): 336; and idem, "Recent Acquisitions, Musée de Cluny, Paris: Tête de Moïse provenant du portail de droite de Saint-Denis," *Gesta* 18 (1989): 107. Yet the identification of the crowned head as that of Moses seems iconographically questionable. In the Benoît drawing of that statue-column from the right portal, the figure generally identified as Moses with the tablet of the Law (Montfaucon, *Les Monumens de la monarchie françoise,* 1: pl. XVIII, upper tier, second from left; and Gerson, *West Facade,* 141) wears not a crown but a close-fitting skullcap with an ornamental design similar to that on the crown of the recently discovered head of a bearded king. The hemline of the adjacent statue-column, the only surviving vestige of that lost figure, has an ornamental border with the identical pattern. Possibly the newly discovered head originally belonged to that figure.

For the statue-column from the cloister, see above, n. 38.

44. Gautier, ms. 11681, 20. Gautier, ibid., 18, also mentioned that in 1770 a scaffolding was erected in front of "the portal" of the abbey; he was probably referring to the central portal, although elsewhere he called the portal either the main door (*porte principale*) of the church or the middle door. Yet in the first instance, since he did not specifically mention the church, he could have meant the twelfth-century "porte de Suger," which was the southwest entrance to the abbey precincts.

45. Guilhermy, ms. 6121, pp. 53–56. For evidence to the contrary, see Chapter 6.

46. For engravings by Fossier of the jambs on the lateral portals that show the restored condition of the sculptures as of 1788—the date of publication of the drawings—see Blum, "Lateral Portals," fig. 3. On both the eighteenth- and nineteenth-century restorations, see ibid., 200–209 and diagrams.

47. Gautier, ms. 11681, 90–93; and idem, *Le Cabinet historique* 21/1 (1875): 39–40.

48. For a general description of Saint-Denis during the revolutionary period, see Louis Réau, *Les Monuments détruits de l'art français,* 1 (Paris, 1959), 224–27, 306–307.

49. In 1844 [Guilhermy], "Saint-Denis. Restauration," 404, attributed the loss of the heads to the revolutionaries.

50. Gautier, ms. 11681, 124. The valves from the lateral portals had been replaced in the 1770–1771 restorations, but those of the central portal were the original bronze doors from Suger's campaign: ibid., 20.

51. See above, n. 42. For an excellent summary of events at Saint-Denis during the revolutionary period, see Paul Vitry and Gaston Brière, *L'Eglise abbatiale royale de Saint-Denis et ses tombeaux. Notice historique et archéologique* (Paris, 1925), 30–34, 103–16; and Crosby, *L'Abbaye royale de Saint-Denis,* 70–71.

52. Gautier, *Le Cabinet historique* 21/1 (1875): 42.

53. François Auguste René Chateaubriand, *Génie du Christianisme, ou beautés de la religion chrétienne,* 2, pt. 4, 7th ed. (Paris, 1822), chap. ix.

54. Commissioner Berche, "Rapport presenté au Ministre de l'Intérieur," dated 11 Messidor an 10 [1802], Folder: "Direction de l'architect Legrand," in "L'Eglise abbatiale de St Denis, an IX [1801]–1811," Paris, Archives Nationales, F^{13} 1293, fol. 27. In

a report concerned with payments due from the "Bâtiments civiles," Berche wrote that one of the minister's predecessors, taking into account the beauties of the architecture and decoration, had decided to conserve the abbey church. The minister had concluded that to render it usable for services it would need an enclosed parish hall.

55. For details of the restorations and alteration of this period, see Paris, Archives Nationales, ibid., F^{13} 1293, 1295, 1296, 1367, summarized in Vitry and Brière, *L'Eglise abbatiale*, 34–37. At the same time the pavement in the nave was raised, but Viollet-le-Duc returned it to the original level; see Crosby (1987), 125.

56. Excavations in 1968 indicated that the original sill of the central portal was 52 cm. below the present pavement level; ibid., 138; and below, Chapter 2, n. 25.

57. Jacques Legrand (1805–1807), Jacques Cellérier (1807–1813), and François Debret (1813–1845). Debret was also the architect of the city of Paris, professor at the Ecole des Beaux-Arts, and a member of the Institute. See *Nouvelles archives de l'art français. Revue de l'art français ancien et modern* (Paris, 1889), 331–34.

CHAPTER 2

1. "The harm is done, and perfectly": Alphonse Didron, *aîné*, "L'Achèvement des restaurations de Saint-Denis," *Annales archéologiques* 5 (1846): 111.

2. Lightning struck the spire of the north tower on 9 June 1837. Debret profited by this accident to acquire new funds which enabled him to rebuild the spire and restore the entire facade: Vitry and Brière, *L'Eglise abbatiale*, 39–40.

3. For an adulatory account of the life and career of the sculptor, see A. Delcourt, *J. S. Brun. Sculpteur statuaire. Ancien pensionnaire de Rome. Saint-Denis. L'Arc de Triomphe de l'Etoile. Le Palais de Justice de Rouen* (Paris, 1846). In addition to the west portals, his restorations at Saint-Denis included the marble statues of Catherine de' Médici; Henri II; the kings, queens, and princes of the house of Valois; and the tomb of Dagobert: ibid., 56–57. He was also involved in the restoration of the sculpture on other medieval monuments, especially in Rouen. Thanks are owing to Elizabeth Brown for this reference.

4. See below, n. 42.

5. "A disfigured facade, deprived forever of historical interest, and, moreover, extremely ugly". Didron, "Achèvement des restaurations," 109.

6. See, inter alia: [Guilhermy], "Saint-Denis. Restauration," 400–411; idem, "Restauration de l'église royale de Saint-Denis," *Annales archéologiques* 5 (1846): 200–215; Didron, "Achèvement des restaurations," ibid., 107–113. Didron and Guilhermy also published numerous articles in the *Annales archéologiques* on aspects of the restorations other than those primarily concerned with the sculpture of the portal: 3 (1844): 245–46; 4 (1845): 175–85, 319–24; 5 (1846): 62–68, 107–113.

7. [Guilhermy], "Saint-Denis. Restauration," 409.

8. Didron, "Achèvement des restaurations," 113.

9. "Rapport sur la restauration de l'église royale de St. Denis [copy]," June, 1841, in

Seine, Saint-Denis, Dossier de l'Administration 1841–1876, Paris, Archives de la Commission des Monuments historiques, fols. 1–12.

10. Debret, "Réponse," fols. 18–22.

11. See "Rapport à l'Académie des Inscriptions et Belles-Lettres et à celle des Beaux-Arts sur la caractère des travaux de restauration exécutés à l'église St Denys, par Mr Debret, Architecte, Membre de l'Institut. 8 avril 1842," ibid., fols. 43–62.

12. Didron, "Achèvement des restaurations," 109: "By the decision of the minister of public works, Monsieur Debret, member of the Institute, architect of the Royal Abbey of Saint-Denis and of the Royal Academy of Music, had been made a member of the Conseil général des bâtiments." To the outrage of Didron, Debret thus joined the supreme committee on architecture that authorized and oversaw all work on public buildings.

13. Didron, ibid., 113, announced the appointment of M. Duban, architect of the Ecole des Beaux-Arts, of the Sainte-Chapelle in Paris, and of the château at Blois.

14. The spire had already been dismantled, but Viollet-le-Duc recommended that the tower also be dismantled to stabilize the weakened westwork: Viollet-le-Duc, "Rapport sur l'état des constructions au 15 Décembre mil huit cent quarante six, 2 janvier 1847," Seine, Saint-Denis, Dossier de l'Administration 1841–1876, Paris, Archives de la Commission des Monuments historiques, fols. 111–13.

15. The Archives Nationales and the Archives de la Commission des Monuments historiques contain the bulk of accounts and records itemizing works undertaken at Saint-Denis.

16. See, inter alia, "La Part de Suger," 91–102, 253–62, 339–49; and Whitney Stoddard, *The West Portals of Saint-Denis and Chartres: Sculpture in the Ile-de-France from 1140–1190* (Cambridge, Mass., 1952), 2–3.

17. For a general outline of work under the direction of Viollet-le-Duc and his successors, see Crosby, *The Abbey of St. Denis,* 10–12; and more recently Crosby (1987), 170, 227–29, 231–32.

18. E. de Labédollière, *Histoire des environs du nouveau Paris* (Paris, ca. 1861), 177–78.

19. The early 1970s saw a campaign to clean the exterior of the church. Aware of the fragility of the sculptures of the western portals, Louis Grodecki was able to convince the authorities of the Monuments historiques not to clean the portals.

20. On the appearance of the three roundels after cleaning, see Blum, "Lateral Portals," 203 and fig. 8.

21. Two unpublished studies have been devoted to a critical examination of the sculptural details of the western portals: a resumé of the thesis of Cécile Goldscheider for the Ecole du Louvre appeared as "Les Origines des portails à statues-colonnes," *Bulletin des musées de France* 6/7 (1946): 22–25; and the doctoral dissertation of Johann Eckart von Borries, "Die Westportale der Abteikirche von Saint-Denis. Versuch einer Rekonstruktion," Ph.D. diss., Universität Hamburg, 1947. Both Mme Goldscheider and Dr. von Borries kindly gave Professor Crosby permission to use their manuscripts in this study.

A third study, by Paula L. Gerson, *The West Facade of St.-Denis. An Iconographic Study,* Ph.D. diss., Columbia University, 1970, Ann Arbor, Mich. (UMI, 1970, no. 73-26, 428), was concerned with iconographical interpretations of the portals. But since this study preceded the completion of the archaeological examination of the central portal, Gerson did not have the benefit of the analysis of the restorations.

22. A shorter version of the results of the examination was first published in France: Sumner McKnight Crosby and Pamela Z. Blum, "Le Portail central de la façade occidentale de Saint-Denis," trans. D. Thibaudat, *Bmon* 131/3 (1973): 209–66. Crosby had previously presented a report summarizing the first, but still preliminary, findings of the 1968 examination of the central portal. Read at the symposium "The Renaissance of the Twelfth Century," held May 14–15, 1969, at the Museum of Art, Rhode Island School of Design, the paper was published as "The West Portals of Saint-Denis and the Saint-Denis Style," *Gesta* 9/2 (1970): 1–11.

23. Erwin Panofsky, "The History of Art as a Humanistic Discipline," in *Meaning in the Visual Arts* (Garden City, N.Y., 1955), 19.

24. The following opinions exemplify conflicts in discussions of style. Whitney Stoddard wrote, "The search for possible origins of the Saint-Denis-Chartres style has led us to Burgundy": Stoddard, *West Portals,* 53. Willibald Sauerländer has maintained, "At Saint-Denis, there is, as far as I can see, no trace of any Burgundian inspiration": Sauerländer, "Sculpture on Early Gothic Churches: The State of Research and Open Questions," *Gesta* 9/2 (1970): 34. He later concluded, "A variety of styles formed the sculptures on the west doorways of Saint-Denis. Though it is now impossible to reach a definite conclusion, the predominating models seem to have come from Toulouse and its sphere of influence": W. Sauerländer, *Gothic Sculpture in France 1140–1270,* trans. J. Sondheimer (New York, 1972), 381.

In 1986 Stoddard emphatically reasserted the Burgundian origins of the Headmaster at Chartres by identifying him with Gislebertus of Autun but suggested that his work at Chartres showed the influence of Saint-Denis—in particular, the influence of the figures of the lost statue-columns: Whitney Stoddard, *The Sculptors of the West Portals of Chartres Cathedral* (New York, London, 1987), 202–209.

25. Recently two articles have presented and discussed all available evidence with respect to the presence or absence of carved lintels in the three portals and the possible heights of the originals: Paula L. Gerson, "The Lintels of the West Facade of Saint-Denis," *Journal of the Society of Architectural Historians* 34 (1975): 189–97; and Kathryn A. Morrison, "The Eighteenth-Century 'Restoration' of the West Portals of Saint-Denis and the Problem of the Lintels," *Journal of the British Archaeological Association* 139 (1986): 134–42 and plates. Using the measurements of the three sets of bronze doors given by Doublet in seventeenth-century *pieds* and comparing them with the heights of the doors today, Gerson computed their original heights by adding the figure of 0.60 m.—the measurement proposed by Viollet-le-Duc as the twelfth-century level of the sills below today's pavement level. With those givens,

Gerson concluded that there had been no lintel under the mosaic in the tympanum of the left portal, one of 0.13 to 0.17 m. under the central portal, and one of circa 0.42 to 0.45 m. under the tympanum of the right portal. But as Crosby noted, Viollet-le-Duc failed to state from what level he had taken his measurement, and since that time, Crosby's excavations have established the sill level at −0.52 m. That measurement proved compatible with Doublet's figures in *pieds*—with the *pied* equaling 0.325 to 0.328 m.: Crosby (1987), 138, 293–94. The correct measurement of the sill level at 0.52 m. below today's pavement modifies Gerson's conclusions and undermines Morrison's assertion that Doublet's measurements in *pieds* were not sufficiently accurate to allow close computations such as Gerson's. Gerson drew her conclusion on the basis of Doublet's figures compared with the widths of the portals today. Morrison assumed that the widths had never been altered, but the archaeological evidence suggests otherwise (see Chapter 6). She therefore found significant discrepancies between the widths today and Doublet's measurements.

In addition, Morrison computed the original heights of the doorways on the basis of 29 cm. as the height of each twelfth-century masonry block in the jambs, whereas the correct measurement is 29.5 cm., the length of the Roman foot (see below, n. 31). Nor does the varying thickness of the mortar from 1 to 3 cm. visible today represent the amount of fill between each masonry block in the jambs, as Morrison supposed, but only superficial repairs of eroded edges along the masonry joints. Finally, Morrison's dismissal of the uppermost blocks of stone on the jambs, or doorposts, of both lateral portals as eighteenth-century additions, not original, is also subject to question. Those masonry blocks and their sculptures appear to be original, but thoroughly recut. Samples of those stones have been taken for spectroanalysis of trace elements to determine definitively whether they came from the same quarry and bed as the rest of the twelfth-century limestone of the jambs. (Spectroanalysis revealed that the tympanum stone of the central portal came from a different quarry.) See also below, n. 31.

Despite questions that have been raised about Morrison's calculations, they nonetheless led her to conclude that all three portals originally had lintels consisting of narrow slabs comparable to the existing one below the tympanum of the central portal. This conclusion accords with the visual evidence provided by the Scamozzi and Martellange drawings (Fig. 2), which offer compelling prerestoration documentation for narrow lintels.

26. Scamozzi's interest in the western portals is recorded in a minute sketch showing the schema of the bronze doors of the central portal as consisting of scenes within medallions. Unfortunately the scenes are indecipherable. See Franco Barbieri, "Vincenzo Scamozzi, studioso ed artista," *Critica d'arte* an. 8, ser. 3, fasc. 19 (1949): fig. 171, and Paris, Arch. Phot. no. 53.N.122. The bronze doors lie outside the scope of this article, but see Gerson, *West Facade*, 100–111; idem, "Suger as Iconographer," in Gerson, ed., *Abbot Suger*, 186–87; and Crosby (1987), 187–92, for interpretations of the visual and textual evidence concerning the iconographical program of the doors.

27. Album Debret, Paris, Archives de la Commission des Monuments historiques. Inasmuch as Debret's *attachements* bear the date 1838 and many details included were never completed, the drawing was probably made in preparation for a presentation to the ministry in support of his request for funds. The details apparently represent what he proposed to do and were not working drawings for the restorers. Similar discrepancies exist between his detail drawings of 1840, which supposedly show work completed (Fig. 5). Guilhermy, ms. 6121, pp. 36, 66, noted that the restoration of the central portal began around 15 September 1839. By October of that year he could write, "On commence le bas relief de la porte gauche modelé par Brun. Le même sculpteur venait de restaurer toutes les voussures de la porte centrale, et commençait à restaurer le bas relief du tympan" (Work is beginning on the bas-relief of the left portal modeled by Brun. The same sculptor has finished restoring all the archivolts of the central portal and is beginning to restore the relief [sculptures] of the tympanum).

28. Diagrams superimposed on photographs proved the most accurate and precise way to summarize the results of the examination. Like any schematic record, they present explicit information, not quantitative and qualitative assessments, such as how severely the surfaces were recut or how accurate the design of the insertion. The text will cover those aspects. Coded so that all original twelfth-century carving can be seen at a glance, the unmarked surfaces represent sculpture untouched by the restoration. Generously spaced crosshatching circumscribed by outlines pinpoints every inset. More closely spaced hatching drawn on the opposite diagonal represents repairs made with mastic, mortar, cement, and gesso. The latter hatching thus maps all repaired fractures, as well as repaired masonry joints impinging upon and distorting the sculpture, even those where some of the mortar fill has crumbled and fallen away. Dotted lines represent fractures that postdate the restoration and have never been repaired. Crossed broken lines designate recut surfaces of twelfth-century stone. That last convention marks every recut area, whether the recutting caused real deformation or simply eliminated minor surface abrasions. For those distinctions, again the reader must rely upon the text.

29. Since the publication of the monograph "Le Portail central," by Crosby and Blum, a considerable number of important studies have appeared concerned with the iconography of the portals. See Paula L. Gerson, "Suger as Iconographer," 183–98; Pamela Z. Blum, "Lateral Portals," 199–228; and Zinn, "Suger, Theology," 33–40; all in Gerson, ed., *Abbot Suger*. See also Charles T. Little, "Monumental Sculpture at Saint-Denis under the Patronage of Abbot Suger," in Crosby et al., *Saint-Denis*, 25–29; Crosby (1987), 179–213; and Conrad Rudolph, *Artistic Change at Saint-Denis: Abbot Suger's Program and the Early Twelfth-Century Controversy over Art* (Princeton, N.J., 1990), especially his chap. 5.

30. Because of the installation of the nineteenth-century pavement 0.52 m. above the twelfth-century level, the lowest bed of masonry visible today appears irregular and completely arbitrary. The original twelfth-century mural masonry continues below the pavement.

Most of the visible blocks of mural masonry are, in fact, original. Stoddard, basing his conclusion on the masonry sloping inward above the level of the decorated plinths and on the depth of the recession, originally posited that every stone and all the carving above the plinths had been cut back 4 cm. in 1839: Stoddard, *West Portals,* 2–3. He later retracted this conclusion after learning the results of the archaeological examination of the central portal: idem, *Sculptors,* 113. Yet no explanation for the recession of the stones of the jambs directly above the plinths seems adequate. Perhaps it represents a peculiarity of the portals, a reflection of difficulties encountered when the masonry of the portals was assembled after the sculptures had been carved in the workshop, or even a tectonic thickening of the structure to strengthen it.

31. The dimension of 29.5 cm. closely approximates the accepted length of the Roman foot: George Forsyth, Jr., *The Church of St. Martin at Angers* (Princeton, N.J., 1953), 23 n. 4. See also below, Chapter 6, n. 2.

    Concerning the masonry of the portals, von Borries, "Die Westportale," 23, stated categorically: "So gibt es heute in linken Sockel des Mittelportals nicht einem einzigen originalen Stein mehr" (So it is today that not a single original stone remains in the left socle [plinth] of the central portal). Although many of the surfaces are badly eroded, the examination indicated that most of the blocks of stone are, in fact, original.

    Selected samples of the twelfth-century stone used for the central and right portals have undergone and been matched by petrographic analysis: C. Jaton and A. Blanc, Rapport, 1973: Dossier, Monument no. 9, Commune Saint-Denis: Fiches prélèvements nos. 93-25 to 93-29. Archives of Sumner McKnight Crosby (uncatalogued), The Cloisters, Fort Tryon Park, New York, N.Y. 10040; and Blum, "Lateral Portals," 221 n. 29.

    Saint-Denis is now the prime monument in a pilot study of French limestones to discover the quarries of their origin. The investigation focuses on trace elements in the stone, determined by thermal neutron activation analysis and collated by multivariate statistics. In addition to resolving problems of attributions of dispersed sculptures, the compositional profiles of the limestone achieved by those analytical procedures will settle problematic aspects of the restorations through sampling to compare the twelfth-century stone with the limestones used by eighteenth- and nineteenth-century restorers. On applications and results of this type of analysis, see, inter alia, Lore L. Holmes, Charles T. Little, and Edward V. Sayre, "Elemental Characterization of Medieval Limestone Sculpture from Parisian and Burgundian Sources," *Journal of Field Archaeology* 13 (1986): 419–38.

32. The fractures may have occurred during the alterations to the portal in 1770–1771, when the trumeau was removed, but more probably in the nineteenth century, when the rebuilding of the north spire caused movement within the masonry of the whole facade.

33. On the exterior surface of the lunette of the upper tympanum, behind an angel's nineteenth-century wing, the end of one of the bolts is visible. On the interior, the heads of the bolts are now obscured by a heavy coat of plaster. A number of holes filled with plaster suggest additional bolts were inserted from the exterior as well. See Chapter 3, "Lunette with Tympanum Angels."

34. See n. 28 above, explaining how the various types of restorations are differentiated in the diagrams.

35. In the Chapter Acts book, in which the canons of Salisbury cathedral transcribed all the plans and specifications of George Gilbert Scott for the restoration of the cathedral in 1876, we find an entry specifying the addition of linseed oil to the mortar used in replacing masonry in the most exposed locations, such as the tower and spire. Scott believed that linseed oil made the mortar impervious to the damaging effects of weather. At Saint-Denis the oil may well have been used for hardening gypsum used to make plaster of Paris, and certainly the oil would have tinted it a buff color.

36. [Guilhermy], "Saint-Denis. Restauration," 407, mentioned that "mastique et la terre cuits" had been used in the restoration of the portals.

37. Guilhermy, ms. 6121, pp. 49, 53, 61, identified the material as "pierre factice." The composite stone appears impervious to weather and acid rain. See also Chapter 6, "The Jamb Colonnettes."

38. Archival records for Saint-Denis contain a payment to M. Dihl (Diehl), maker of *mastic imperméable:* "L'Eglise abbatiale de Saint-Denis, 1811–1822," Paris, Archives Nationales, F^{13} 1295, fol. 76, as well as numerous references to the use of mastic in the early nineteenth-century restorations and alterations. In one instance, the formula, which included linseed oil, seems to have produced a mastic used for coating the walls in the crypt to prevent dampness from penetrating the stone: ibid., F^{13} 1296, fol. 100. In his discussion of restorations to French buildings, Paul Léon, *La Vie des monuments français. Destruction. Restauration* (Paris, 1951), 366, wrote: "Later Debret in the work at the basilica of Saint-Denis, [and] Godde in the churches of Paris, authorized the facing of masonry by extraordinary materials, the mastic of Diehl, the cement of Molesmes or of Wasy, which, thanks to the quick and uniform scraping [of the stones], gave a new appearance to the most degraded monuments."

39. On the extent of the eighteenth-century work and aspects distinguishing it from the nineteenth-century restoration, see Blum, "Lateral Portals," 200–202.

40. Von Borries, "Die Westportale," 116–17. See also Arch. Phot., Paris, no. 83675. For a possible explanation of the function of the fragment, see the ornamental animal-head finials, typical embellishments of bench ends that rise above the level of the seat: Eugène Viollet-le-Duc, *Dictionnaire raisonné du mobilier français de l'époque carlovingienne à la renaissance,* 1, *Meubles* (Paris, 1871), "Bancs," 33–34. See Bildarchiv Foto Marburg no. 36991, and Arch. Phot., Paris, nos. 11471, 83627.

41. Nevertheless, as noted above, the accounts indicate that Brun alone restored the figures. He had considerable assistance, mainly for restorations to and replacement of

ornament, from the workshop of le Sieur (or Monsieur) Blois, which also executed the twenty large columns decorated with abstract vegetal and geometric designs carved to replace the statue-columns; 686 cm. of new decorative friezes to frame the Signs of the Zodiac on the jambs of the left portal; the recutting and restoration of 703 cm. of the great foliate frieze that surrounds the central portal; and the nineteenth-century additions of both figurate and ornamental sculptures to the upper stages of the west facade: Blois, "L'Eglise royale de St. Denis. Etat des dépenses . . . ," Seine, Saint-Denis, Registre des attachements de l'église royale de Saint-Denis, "Statuaire et Sculpture, 1835–1842," Paris, Archives de la Commission des Monuments historiques, Carton 27.

CHAPTER 3

1. "Le Christ présidant au jugement dernier porte aujourd'hui . . . la tête de Jupiter Olympien": [Guilhermy], "Saint-Denis. Restauration," 404.
2. The piercing of Christ's side by the spear of Longinus, the believing soldier, is found in the apocryphal Passion Gospel known as the Gospel of Nicodemus, or Acts of Pilate (16:7). See Montague Rhodes James, ed. and trans., *The Apocryphal New Testament, Being the Apocryphal Gospels, Acts, Epistles, and Apocalypses with Other Narratives and Fragments* (Oxford, 1963), 113.
3. Comparable examples of this type of throne can be found in Ottonian and Carolingian miniatures and ivories. For two Ottonian examples, see Adolph Goldschmidt, *Die Elfenbeinskulpturen aus der Zeit der karolingischen und sächsischen Kaiser*, 1 (Paris, 1914), pl. LXXIV, fig. 162; II (1918), pl. VI, fig. 16.
4. In an excellent iconographical study of the west portals of Saint-Denis, Gerson interpreted the figure of Christ with arms outstretched before the cross and with only the lower portions of his body surrounded by a mandorla as imagery derived from the Augustinian argument concerning the dual nature of Christ as the Son of God and as the Son of man. In reconciling the conflicting evidence in the Gospels of John and Matthew concerning the presence of Christ at the Last Judgment (Matthew 25:31–32; John 12:47), St. Augustine developed the concept that Christ the Son of man would judge the wicked, and, at the same time, the good would see him in his divine form as the Son of God: *De Trinitate* 1, 13, 31, *P.L.* 42, cols. 843–44. Gerson concluded that the upper portion of Christ before the cross represented his image as the Son of man come to judge, and the lower portion of the figure in glory depicted his divine nature: Gerson, *West Facade,* 119–25.

   Gerson also emphasized the special significance to Suger of the image of the crucified Christ, not the least because of the association of the Crucifixion with the conversion of Dionysius the Areopagite (Acts 17:22–34). When preaching in Athens, St. Paul saw an altar erected by the Athenians to an unknown god. He explained that without knowing it, the Athenians were worshiping his God. On hearing Paul preaching and disputing on the Areopagus, Dionysius came to believe. From the ninth century on, after the Areopagite, the disciple of St. Paul, and St. Denis were deemed one and the same, legendary embellishments greatly expanded the biblical episode. According to these later accounts, the erection of the altar on the Areopagus was said to have resulted from an awesome three-hour eclipse of the sun. Thereafter the Athenians erected the altar in the belief that an unknown god of Nature had died, and that the eclipse signified Nature mourning. Paul explained to them that the unknown god they had honored was Christ, and the three-hour eclipse that could not be explained by natural causes had occurred at the time of his Crucifixion. For the fully developed legend, see Granger Ryan and Helmut Ripperger, eds., *The Golden Legend of Jacobus de Voragine* (New York, 1969), 617–20; for the ninth-century text, Hincmar, *Miracula Sancti Dionysii*, in *Acta sanctorum ordinis Benedicti*, ed. Jean Mabillon, saeculum 3, pt. 2 (Paris, 1772), 343–64.

For Gerson's illuminating analysis of Suger as an iconographer and the importance of the Crucifixion to his beliefs as revealed by his writing and by the imagery in the decoration of the abbey, see especially, Gerson, *West Facade*, 57–75; and more recently, idem, "Suger as Iconographer," 183–86. Zinn, "Suger, Theology," 33–37, has established the relationship between Suger's programs and the treatises of Hugh of Saint-Victor, one of the outstanding theologians of that time—especially Hugh's commentary on Dionysius the Pseudo-Areopagite's *Celestial Hierarchy*. Recently Conrad Rudolph, *Artistic Change*, 32–47, has posited that Suger, admittedly not a theologian, was incapable of formulating the sophisticated iconographical programs of the portals and the windows, but had relied instead on Hugh of Saint-Victor to create them. Rudolph saw the conflation of Augustinian ideas with those of Dionysius the Pseudo-Areopagite in the imagery of the central portal as a perfect expression of Hugh's theology.

A critique of Rudolph's hypothesis concerning Hugh's active participation in the programs for the portals and windows lies outside the scope of this study, but if one postulates that Suger knew Hugh's treatises, Hugh's actual participation would seem unnecessary. We should also bear in mind the words of Suger's contemporary, his secretary and biographer Willelmus of Saint-Denis, a work Rudolph himself quoted: "In him [Suger] flourished not only a natural felicity of memory, but also the highest art of understanding what had to be done and taking heed to such a degree that he held in readiness whatever exceptional things he either had heard said or had said himself at one time or another for the place and time [that they should be needed]": ibid., 33; and Willelmus, *Litterae encyclicae conventus Sancti Dionysii de morte Sugerii abbatis*, in *Oeuvres complètes de Suger*, ed. Auguste Lecoy de la Marche (Paris, 1867), 405–406. But see also Peter Kidson, "Panofsky, Suger, and St Denis," *J.W.C.I.* 50 (1987), 1–17. Rudolph's arguments take up where Kidson's revisionistic essay minimizing Suger's role as patron left off. In concluding, Kidson wrote that "Suger was not in any serious sense a follower of the Pseudo-Dionysius. . . . As for the Pseudo-Dionysius, if he had anything to do with twelfth-century religious art, it was through the exegetical movement associated (among others) with the canons of

St Victor, rather than St Denis. This might provide a starting point for further inquiry into Suger's alleged role as one of the great innovators of medieval iconography": ibid., 17.

5. Notable examples of exactly this type of articulated cross occur in the second crucifix of Abbess Matilda from Essen, dated between 974 and 1101: Emma Medding-Alp, *Rheinische Goldschmeidekunst in ottonischer Zeit* (Koblenz, 1952), fig. 36; and in London, Brit. Lib. Stowe Ms. 944, fol. 6, dated between 1020 and 1030, showing King Cnut and his wife Ælfgyfu presenting an altar cross: Margaret Rickert, *Painting in Britain: The Middle Ages,* 2nd ed. (Harmondsworth and Baltimore, 1965), pl. 37A.

6. Guilhermy, ms. 6121, p. 63.

7. "Come, ye blessed of my Father" and "Depart from me, you cursed." All biblical quotations are taken from the Vulgate (Douay edition), the version of the Bible closest to the one used in the twelfth century.

8. Guilhermy, ms. 6121, pp. 62–64; and [idem], "Saint-Denis. Restauration," 404.

9. For examples of the Last Judgment that included those verses from Matthew, see, inter alia, the Last Judgment tympanum at Conques: Gustav Künstler, ed., *Romanesque Art in Europe* (Greenwich, Conn., 1968), pl. 39; the Freckenhorst baptismal font: Erwin Panofsky, *Die Deutsche Plastik des elften bis dreizehnten Jahrhunderts,* repr. (New York, 1969), pl. 16; a badly worn Carolingian ivory in London, Victoria and Albert Museum: Goldschmidt, *Elfenbeinskulpturen,* I, pl. LXXIII, fig. 178; and the Gunhild Crucifix in the Copenhagen National Museum: ibid., III, pl. XLIV, fig. 124b. For other examples, see also Gerson, "Suger as Iconographer," 196 n. 22. Although Christ of the tympanum at Saint-Denis is viewed in the literature as Christ of the Last Judgment, the Judgment proper is actually taking place in the center of the first archivolt. See Chapter 4, "The Judging Christ."

10. A great deal more has survived in the Resurrection frieze than von Borries's study suggested. He noted that the figures had been heavily restored. Then, calling the figures "nineteenth-century," he stated that too little remained to allow any reconstruction of the original work: von Borries, "Die Westportale," 119. Quite the contrary proved true.

11. Suger, *De administratione,* in Panofsky, ed., *Suger,* 48–49. Unaware of evidence to the contrary, von Borries, "Die Westportale," 119–20, called the pose of the figure an invention of the eighteenth or nineteenth century.

12. Through the centuries, the classical symbolism associated with the goddess Persephone clung to the pomegranate, and in Christian iconography it came to signify resurrection and the hope of immortality: George Ferguson, *Signs and Symbols in Christian Art* (New York, 1961), 37. In the mid-thirteenth century, the pomegranate is carried by one of the Blessed in the Last Judgment scene on the central portal of the cathedral of Saint-Etienne at Bourges. The attribute held by the bishop or king in the Resurrection frieze at Saint-Denis may be a precocious example of the vegetal and floral symbolism so prevalent in the sculptural ensembles on thirteenth-century cathedral portals. In Christian iconography the pomegranate

also signifies the church. The medieval mind, which delighted in multiple layers of meaning, would have considered this symbol particularly appropriate in the hand of a resurrected bishop at the Last Judgment. Unfortunately the attribute does not resolve the identity of the figure because its symbolism seems no less appropriate to the figure of a resurrected king in the tympanum of the royal abbey. Though a small iconographical detail, the pomegranate carried by a king would dovetail perfectly with Abbot Suger's aspirations to associate his abbey with the monarchy in the eyes of his contemporaries.

13. The heads were reproduced in Marcel Aubert and Michèle Beaulieu, *Musée National du Louvre. Description raisonée des sculptures,* 1, *Moyen Age* (Paris, 1950), 57, nos. 52, 53, 54, 55. (No. 56, also described as having come from Saint-Denis and grouped with the above, quite obviously belongs to a later period and is a head from one of the marmosets in the Porte des Valois.) See also Crosby, *L'Abbaye royale de Saint-Denis,* 34–35 nos. 6–9; and Chapter 7 of this study.

14. See below, Chapter 7, n. 2.

15. The Louvre double heads no. 54 and those of Apostles nos. 21 and 22 measure 0.16 m. along the diagonal break and 0.155 m. on a horizontal line drawn under their beards. In both cases, the angle drawn from the upper right end along the break to meet an imaginary horizontal drawn from the lower or left edge equals 20 degrees. The heights of the heads, measured from the tops to the tips of the beards, correlate closely with the nineteenth-century restorations:

| Louvre head, left | 0.18 m. | Louvre head, right | 0.145 m. |
| Apostle no. 21 | 0.185 m. | Apostle no. 22 | 0.13 m. |

The greatest depth of the Louvre heads along the break measures 0.085 m. The greatest projection of the twelfth-century bodies measured along the joint is 0.10 m. The correspondence of those critical measurements along the break and the joint indicates a perfect congruence.

16. St. Augustine stated, "Qui enim disputat, verum discernit a falso" (Who in fact disputes, discerns truth from falsehood): *Contra Cresconium grammaticum partis Donati,* I, 15, 19, *P.L.* 43, col. 457. In regard to the dialogue, see especially Fritz Saxl, "Frühes Christentum und spätes Heidentum in ihren künsterlischen Ausdruckformen," 1: "Der Dialog als Thema der christlichen Kunst," *Wiener Jahrbuch für Kunstgeschichte* n.f. 2 (16) (1923): 64–77. The bas-relief discovered at Saint-Denis during the excavations of 1947 provides another example from Suger's workshops of the Apostles *in disputatione:* Sumner McKnight Crosby, *The Apostle Bas-Relief at Saint-Denis* (New Haven, Conn., 1972), 53; and on the antique theme of philosopher and student (or poet and muse) that was the prototype for the convention of the apostolic dialogue: ibid., 63–64.

17. Von Borries, "Die Westportale," 111–12. The Virgin's gesture derives from classical art, in particular from images on grave stellae depicting the woman's hand drawing the edge of the veil covering her head toward her face, as if about to conceal it. The language of gesture has great significance in medieval representations and can often

supply the clue to the meaning of an obscure scene. As R. W. Scheller noted, "The medieval method of illustrating man's relationships with his fellow men consisted of a symbolic language of gestures couched in specific formulas": *A Survey of Medieval Model Books* (Haarlem, 1963), 32. Usually associated with the Crucifixion, in this Last Judgment scene the Virgin's mourning gesture certainly refers to Christ's Crucifixion—a reference evoked by the figure of Christ with arms outstretched before the cross and by the symbols of his Passion carried by the attending angels. The Virgin as a suppliant for mankind seems implicit both in her pose and by her presence. If so, the role of Mary as advocate for sinners is an important iconographical detail. She appeared a very few years earlier (ca. 1135) enthroned at the Last Judgment in the tympanum at Autun, but there her gesture should probably be interpreted as one of adulation rather than supplication or mourning. For an illustration and identification of that figure, see Denis Grivot and George Zarnecki, *Gislebertus, Sculptor of Autun* (New York, 1961), 26, plan I and pl. M. In both literature and art, as the cult of the Virgin developed and reached its apogee in the next century, Mary as the intermediary for disparate causes became a favored theme.

Among the numerous examples of the Virgin mourning at the Crucifixion and holding her veil in her left hand is a ninth-century ivory book cover on a missal from Saint-Denis now in the Bibliothèque Nationale, Paris (ms. lat. 9436). For an illustration, see Danielle Gaborit-Chopin, *Ivoires du Moyen Age* (Fribourg, Switzerland, 1978), fig. 78.

18. [Guilhermy], "Saint-Denis. Restauration," 404–405.

19. For earlier examples of the Deisis where John parallels the mourning Virgin by making the same gesture, see Goldschmidt, *Elfenbeinskulpturen,* I, pl. XLVII, fig. 100; II, pl. XVII, figs. 55 and 57; III, pl. VII, fig. 23.

20. Despite the lack of definitive evidence, Gerson, *West Facade,* 125–26, agreed that the original arrangement probably represented the western form of the Deisis. She suggested that Suger's inclusion of the figures of the Virgin and John the Evangelist with the Last Judgment resulted from his preoccupation with the Crucifixion and therefore did not represent a borrowing from and variation on the Byzantine Last Judgment, where traditionally the Virgin and John the Baptist were the intercessors. Gerson also cited the presence of the Virgin and John the Evangelist in the Last Judgment of Saint-Maur (Huy), in a tympanum generally dated in the first half of the twelfth century. Because of the imprecise dating, the order of precedence remains unresolved.

21. Von Borries, "Die Westportale," 117.

22. Von Borries, ibid., 113–14, mistakenly concluded that the nineteenth-century restoration had completely rearranged the first three Apostles, thereby eliminating Apostle no. 22.

23. See Cambridge, Eng., Pembroke College Ms. 120, fol. 6. Dated between 1120 and 1140, the miniature depicting the Pentecost shows an arrangement of the Apostles' feet that suggests this amusing conceit: Catalogue, *L'Art Roman. Exposition orga-*

nisée par le gouvernement espagnol sous les auspices du Conseil de l'Europe (Barcelona and Santiago de Compostela, 1961), pl. 12, no. 177.

24. The severest recutting occurred on the torso, right arm, left leg, and fluttering scarf of trumpeting angel no. 20; around both knees of Apostle no. 21; on the right knee of Apostle no. 28; on the right shoulder of Apostle no. 31; and on the far left and right of the angel with the flaming sword, particularly on his lower right-sleeve drapery, left shoulder, and upper arm. In the figures listed, inept carving of the stone patches also mars the visual effect of the drapery. The recut, rough area on the upper torso of Apostle no. 26 resulted from the cutting-away of his mutilated, twelfth-century right hand, which apparently rested on his chest. The fracture of the tympanum stone that invades his figure caused considerable damage, now repaired with mortar as well as recutting.

25. The accurate and close-up view permitted by the scaffolding makes it necessary to reconsider an idea presented earlier—that the angel might have been carrying a "coussin avec les Trois Clous (a cushion with the three nails)": Crosby, *L'Abbaye royale de Saint-Denis,* 37. Commenting on the probable iconography of Suger's Great Cross, Philippe Verdier emphasized the precocious appearance at Saint-Denis of the crucified Christ represented with his feet overlapping, an arrangement requiring three rather than four nails. He cited the quotation above to support the possibility that the central tympanum contained another representation involving only three nails. The fact that the nineteenth-century insert had four nails does not guarantee that four were originally represented. Although probable, they lack verification, which leaves Verdier's hypothesis an open question: Verdier, "La Grande Croix de l'Abbé Suger à Saint-Denis," *Cahiers de civilisation médiévale Xe–XIIe siècles* 13 (1970): 3 n. 9, 4 n. 10.

26. The relics of the Passion were received at the abbey in the ninth century. According to legend, they were removed from Aix-la-Chapelle by Charles the Bald, who supposedly gave them to Saint-Denis in 862. Suger mentioned the relics in three different places and always referred to the nail in the singular: Suger, *De consecratione,* II and IV; idem, *Ordinatio,* in Panofsky, ed., *Suger,* 87, 101, 133.

27. Von Borries, "Die Westportale," 101, identified the attribute as a "Kasten" (chest or coffer) and gave no further explanation. He also described the four angels as the best-preserved figures in the tympanum.

28. The lost cross of St. Eloi, a golden and bejeweled gift to Saint-Denis from Dagobert, is known today primarily through inventories of the abbey and the detailed rendering of the cross in the late fifteenth-century painting *The Mass of Saint Giles.* According to the inventories, at the base of the cross an enameled reliquary protected by glass contained a fragment of the True Cross. The painting shows that the crystal covering the fragment bears the label "de cruce d[omi]ni." Despite the use of that abbreviated form of *domini* in both the seventh and thirteenth centuries, the Gothic script of the label indicates that at the earliest, the relic was a thirteenth-century addition. Suger mentioned "illam ammirabilem sancti Eligii . . . crucem," but

167

never listed a relic of the True Cross among the treasures of the abbey: Suger, *De administratione,* in Panofsky, ed., *Suger,* 62. Since the fragment postdates Suger's workshops, the object carried by angel no. III may accurately replace the original attribute, but the original could not have been a reference to a relic not yet in the abbey's possession. See W. Martin Conway, "The Abbey of Saint-Denis and Its Ancient Treasures," *Archaeologia* 66, 2nd ser. (1915): 125, pl. II, and bibliography; also Comte Blaise de Montesquiou-Fezensac, "Nouvelles observations sur la croix de Saint-Eloi au trésor de Saint-Denis," *Bulletin de la Société nationale des Antiquaires de France* (1967): 229–30; and idem, "Une Epave du trésor de Saint-Denis," in *Mélanges en hommage à la mémoire de Fr. Martroye* (Paris, 1940), 289–301, identifying a fragment of the cross of St. Eloi now in the Cabinet des Médailles, Paris, Bibliothèque Nationale.

29. See above, Chapter 2, n. 33.

30. The initials could be those of the sculptor Blois, who assisted Brun with the foliate ornament. Never including his given name, the work sheets always refer to him as Le Sieur Blois (an alternative to "Monsieur").

CHAPTER 4

1. Von Borries, "Die Westportale," 22–24, believed that the blessing gesture of the right hand followed the twelfth-century design but suggested that the left hand, which he read as an *Orantengestus* (the orans gesture of prayer used in ancient and Early Christian times), had originally held the *Liber Vitae* (Apocalypse 20:12).

   Recently Rudolph, *Artistic Change,* 41–42, wrote that in the central portal "Christ makes no gesture of approval or of condemnation," and that there is no act of separation of the Elect and the Damned, no scales and weighing of souls, and that Judgment is not specifically portrayed as being in progress. Certainly Rudolph's statement holds true for the tympanum, but not for the Christ in the first archivolt, center. Rudolph went on to suggest that there Christ is blessing both souls that flank him. Yet in Christian art, with no known exception, the gesture of blessing is always made with the right hand. To interpret the gesture made with the left hand as one of blessing runs counter to iconographical tradition. Furthermore, below the Judging Christ, we see the consequences of his Judgment: the Blessed in Paradise on his right and the Damned tumbling toward Hell on his left; see also below, n. 2.

2. Rudolph, ibid., 41, suggested that the two souls represented "those who are not judged, but saved"—a reference to Gregory the Great's *Moralia in Job,* wherein there were two subdivisions for the elect: those who were judged and saved and those not judged but saved, with similar subdivisions obtaining for the Damned. Rudolph stressed the importance of Gregory's writings to Hugh of Saint-Victor, whom the author saw as the iconographer responsible for the program of the central portal. See above, Chapter 3, n. 4.

   Zinn, "Suger, Theology," 37, has linked the images in the center archivolts and tympanum with a lost drawing by Hugh of Saint-Victor, which we know only from

Hugh's description of it in *De arca Noe mystica,* 2, 15, *P.L.* 176, cols. 701–702. Hugh depicted Christ holding a disk representing the cosmos that hid all but his head, hands, and feet. At his feet the Last Judgment was depicted with the Saved on the right and the Damned on the left, accompanied by the texts of Matthew 25:34 and 41. Although compositional parallels with the images in the third archivolt, center, are striking, the imagery at Saint-Denis differs in that the Deity, not Christ, is holding the cosmological disk, and it contains the *signum Christi.* See below, nn. 6–7.

3. Bildarchiv Foto Marburg no. 36999 clearly shows the drapery reworked with mastic.

4. In keeping with his suggestion that the keystone of the first archivolt depicted a variant on the *Maiestas Domini,* von Borries, "Die Westportale," 132–33, suggested that the angels originally held a crown.

5. The absence of embellishments is puzzling, since the Deity depicted in the keystone of the outer archivolt of the left, or north portal has a jeweled nimbus, as does Christ in the tympanum of the south portal. See Blum, "The Lateral Portals," figs. 9, 16.

6. On this and earlier representations of the Trinity, see Gerson, *West Facade,* 129–36; idem, "Suger as Iconographer," 192–94; and Zinn, "Suger, Theology," 37. Both Gerson and Zinn assumed that the feet of the Deity were valid insertions, as did Conrad Rudolph, in a paper delivered in Washington, D.C., at the 1991 meeting of the College Art Association. Following Zinn (see above, n. 2), Rudolph associated the Trinity at Saint-Denis with the description of the lost cosmic schema in Hugh of Saint-Victor's treatise, *De arca Noe mystica.* Rudolph's paper represented a portion of a study in preparation on the iconography of the three western portals of Saint-Denis.

As Gerson noted, the center archivolts contain the first known appearance of the Trinity in monumental sculpture: "Suger as Iconographer," 192. Gerson interpreted the image of the Trinity surrounded by the twenty-four elders of the Apocalypse in Augustinian terms. Together they represented "the ultimate state of grace at the end of time," or "the final salvation," made possible by Christ's sacrifice on the cross.

For a twelfth-century example (ca. 1170) of a cosmic schema, see that of Hildegard von Bingen (1098–1179), from *De operatione Dei,* wherein the entire universe is in the bosom of the Creator; see Matthew Fox, *Illuminations of Hildegard of Bingen* (Santa Fe, N.M., 1985), 38. See also the Trinity in Hildegard's *Liber Scivias,* where she illustrated the "New Heaven, New Earth"—an apocalyptic vision as pictured in her book written between 1140 and 1150. The lowest of three circles represents all the cosmic processes, the middle ring contains the builders of Zion, patriarchs, prophets, Apostles, martyrs, confessors and virgins, and above, in the uppermost circle, the Trinity is represented by the Deity, enthroned, holding a disk containing the Lamb and cross, and above that circle, a nimbed Dove: Fox, *Illuminations,* 110.

Von Borries, "Die Westportale," 130–31, correctly noted that the feet of the Deity were modern, but he erred in stating that the medallion and the Lamb were also nineteenth-century restorations. Von Borries cited the Apocalypse of Saint-Sever as the iconographical source for the Trinity in the central archivolts.

7. Gertrud Schiller, *Iconography of Christian Art,* 2, trans. J. Seligman (London, 1972), 118.

8. "[The restorer] profited, I have been assured, by the slightest indications [of the original work] such as the feet of the dove": Guilhermy, ms. 6121, p. 66.

9. "Not a stone escaped the hand of the workers": Didron, "Achèvement des restaurations," 108. Originally the entire face, nose included, was accepted as original, which no longer seems credible in view of the distinct line of corrosion that has developed across the ridge and continues partway down the left side of the nose. Distinguishable in photographs from the weathering of the stone proper, the difference may indicate a line of mortar or cement joining a modern nose. For the earlier conclusion, see Crosby and Blum, "Le Portail central," 236.

CHAPTER 5

1. "Some indications survived which . . . [the restorer] has followed": Guilhermy, ms. 6121, pp. 64, 66. Von Borries, "Die Westportale," 127–29, 153, did not accept the scenes of Hell as restored. He considered all of them a nineteenth-century invention and concluded that the twelfth-century scenes had been completely obliterated. He proposed that originally there had been a tripartite arrangement paralleling the scenes of Paradise on the left, namely: Hell at the bottom, a cauldron with fire in the second, and in the third tier, four figures depicting the punishments of the Damned. He cited as reference the fragments of the scenes of Hell from Notre-Dame-de-Corbeil now in the Louvre.

2. Von Borries saw traces of original carving in this figure: ibid., 126–27.

3. On the Wise and Foolish Virgins as a theme forging a link with the imagery on Suger's lost bronze doors, the inscription on the lintel, as well as the sculptures on the jambs, inner archivolt, and tympanum, see Gerson, "Suger as Iconographer," 187–88.

4. Another classical motif occurs on the right jamb of the left, or north portal. Below the sign of Gemini at the top of the jamb, in a frame decorated with the scroll motif, a stylized flower resembles the type that filled the center of compartments in coffered ceilings in ancient Greece, as for example the ceiling of the interior corridor of the Tholos at Epidauros.

CHAPTER 6

1. Vitry and Brière, *L'Eglise abbatiale,* 61, suggested that the jambs of all three portals looked as if their restorations predated the nineteenth century. The archeological examination has, in part, verified their conclusion, but it was also necessary to distinguish between the eighteenth- and nineteenth-century work, for without doubt, both periods left their mark on the jambs. On this question, see also Blum, "Lateral Portals," 200–206.

2. As noted, the measurement of 29.5 cm. equals the length of the Roman foot. The

occurrence of that measurement in the masonry of all three portals and the rare, if not unique, use of it here in a building of the Ile-de-France offers but one of many pieces of evidence that have led me to conclude that the workshops of sculptors gathered by Suger contained an artist from Italy—not only one from Italy, but one trained in the workshop of Niccolò. An essay on the stylistic sources of the western portals is in preparation, and it will fully document that hypothesis as well as point to strong influences traceable to an atelier of ivory workers located in Cologne. To date, scholars have emphasized stylistic influences from the Languedoc, western France, and Burgundy. See also below, Chapter 8, n. 5.

3. See above, Chapter 2, n. 42.

4. Guilhermy, ms. 6121, p. 62; von Borries, "Die Westportale," 88.

5. See Crosby and Blum, "Le Portail central," 242–43. According to Guilhermy, ms. 1621, p. 62, all eight heads of the virgins on the jambs were redone in 1840, as well as a number of hands. He also reported that the restorer followed the indications provided by the original vestiges to determine whether they should be bareheaded or veiled.

6. Morrison attributed the cropping to the 1770–1771 restorations. See above, Chapter 2, n. 25.

7. Similar alterations and cropping occurred in the west portals of Chartres cathedral. Accommodations required during the assemblage and installation of the sculpture are especially noticeable in the south tympanum.

8. The parallels continue in the crossed legs of the Atlantids but cease in the matter of the large head that dwarfs the body. In addition, the ornament flanking his body lies on the background plane rather than forming a frame or niche. For an illustration, see Arturo C. Quintavalle, *Romanico Padano, Civiltà d'Occidente* (Florence, 1969), 292, fig. 133.

9. See Jurgis Baltrušaitis, "Villes sur arcatures," *Urbanisme et architecture. Etudes écrites et publiées en l'honneur de Pierre Lavadan* (Paris, 1954): 31–40.

10. At Saint-Denis, other examples of monsters occur on the middle capital of the left embrasure of the south portal, west facade; on the corbel attached to the southeastern face of the engaged compound pier, north wall of the western bays; and on the southeastern hemicycle pier in the crypt (recut in the nineteenth century).

11. On the motif, see Crosby, *Apostle Bas-Relief,* 35.

12. Guilhermy, ms. 6121, p. 61.

13. Von Borries, "Die Westportale," 92, condemned the entire figure as a replacement.

14. Guilhermy, ms. 6121, p. 62.

15. Camille Enlart, *Manuel d'archéologie française 3, Le Costume* (Paris, 1916), 606.

16. Guilhermy, ms. 6121, pp. 49–50. Divided in two, with modern bases and capitals added, the original shaft from which the colonnette now on the right jamb of the central portal was molded was transferred to the Musée de Cluny from the Louvre in 1955 (inv. no. L.S. RF 45253). There it joined the column (inv. no. 19576) from which the modern shaft now on the left jamb of the portal was molded. See Marcel

Aubert et al., *Cathédrales* (Musée du Louvre) (Paris, 1962), 23, nos. 1–2. The former originally came from the right jamb of the north portal, and the latter from the right jamb of the south portal. Both had been dismounted in the nineteenth century to make an altar *jubé*. Guilhermy, ms. 1621, p. 61, correctly described the extant nineteenth-century colonnettes of the central portal as "moulées sur celles des autels du jubé." Elsewhere in his notes he described the *jubé* columns as "provenant de la façade," and decorated "avec feuillages, bandeaux et signes de zodise": ibid., "Autels du jubé [1827–1830]," p. 130. The date of his observations indicates that the colonnettes were removed about a decade before Brun began his restorations. Stoddard has summarized the history of the original columns and other fragments now in the Cluny: *West Portals*, 4–5, pls. V–VI.

When in the Louvre, both halves of the colonnette from the left portal still had the nineteenth-century bases and capitals that adapted them for the altar *jubé*. See Aubert and Beaulieu, *Description raisonée . . . ,* vol. I, *Moyen Age,* fig. 57. At the Cluny, the bases were removed and the two pieces rejoined. Recently a newly carved midsection was inserted to increase the height of the shaft to equal that of the other Cluny colonnette originally from the right portal. The inset was an error, in that the left doorway is smaller than the right, and the colonnettes should reflect that difference.

17.   Guillaume Le Gentil de la Galaisière, "Observations sur plusieurs monumens gothiques . . . sur lesquels sont gravés les signes du zodiaque et quelques hiéroglyphes egyptiens relatifs à la religion d'Isis," *Histoire de l'Académie royale des Sciences, 1788 . . .* (Paris, 1791): 397–438, pls. XVII–XVIII. More recently May Vieillard-Troïekouroff, "Les Zodiaques parisiens sculptés d'après Le Gentil de la Galaisière, astronome du XVIIIe siècle," *Mémoires de la Société nationale des Antiquaires de France* 4, 9e ser., 1968 (Paris, 1969): 161–94, figs. 8–9. Von Borries, "Die Westportale," 36–37, also mentioned the drawings.

Unaware of the engravings, Stoddard assigned two other fragments of colonnettes from Saint-Denis in Cluny reserve (inv. no. 11659a–b) to the embrasures of the Saint-Denis portals and posited their original disposition in an arrangement similar to the decorated shafts or intercolonnettes between the statue columns of the western portals of Chartres cathedral: *West Portals*, 6–7, pl. VI, fig. 2. Von Borries, "Die Westportale," 31–32, concluded that no fragments of the colonnettes of the central portal were known, but suggested that some might be found at the Musée de Cluny. In fact, the fragments mentioned above and two others in the reserve all originally belonged to the lateral portals. See below, nn. 18–19.

18.   The fragment in question (Musée de Cluny, inv. no. 11659a) formed the lower half of the colonnette pictured in the engravings published by Le Gentil de la Galaisière on the left jamb of the right portal and illustrated in Stoddard, *West Portals,* pl. VI 2 (right). Both show the face of the fragment originally oriented to the west. Not pictured by Stoddard, the right or south face of that segment is particularly attractive and less restored. The vertical rinceau is inhabited by three nude figures wielding

various weapons: a club, a bow and arrow, and what may be a boomerang. That face of the shaft with its vertically organized ornament has never been published.

M. Alain Erlande-Brandenburg kindly made arrangements for me to examine the fragment after the dust and dirt that covered it had been removed. The washing that he authorized revealed many passages of twelfth-century sculpture, as well as several kinds of repairs. The visually disconcerting style in some areas resulted from drastic and stylistically incompatible recutting and also from insertions of small, nineteenth-century elements, some carved in stone, others molded in plaster. The numerous restorations will be diagrammed and analyzed in an article in preparation.

19. The Cluny reserve has three more fragments of the colonnettes used in the altar *jubés,* one of which appears to have been entirely a nineteenth-century fabrication. Le Gentil's engraving of the left portal shows the original location for two of the fragments on the left jamb of the left portal. The best preserved of the two (inv. no. 11569b) is illustrated in Stoddard, *West Portals,* pl. VI 2 (left). In the 1970s all colonnette fragments from Saint-Denis were moved from Paris to the Cluny reserve at Château Ecouen, north of Paris. Although now stripped of all nineteenth-century additions, the shafts had been heavily and clumsily restored, newly carved insets added to the ends, their designs continued onto the uncarved back surfaces, and bases and capitals added.

20. For an analysis of this type of ornamentation, see Crosby, *Apostle Bas-Relief.*

21. For illustrations of those decorated shafts, see Stoddard, *West Portals,* pls. XII–XVIII, XXVI, XXIX, XXXVII. The motif of the inhabited vine or scrolls also has affinities with the capitals from Saint-Etienne and La Daurade in Toulouse; ibid., pl. XXXI. The origins of the motif, however, are usually traced to England or Germany: Lawrence Stone, *Sculpture in Britain. The Middle Ages* (Harmondsworth, 1955), 62; Fritz Saxl, *English Sculptures of the Twelfth Century,* ed. H. Swarzenski (Boston, 1952), n. 4, fig. 25; and George Zarnecki, Janet Holt, and Tristram Holland, eds., *English Romanesque Art 1066–1200* (London, 1984), 215, cat. nos. 184–185; 217, cat. no. 189.

22. Von Borries, "Die Westportale," 19–20, like all earlier scholars, assumed that lintels originally existed under all three portals. Also see above, Chapter 2, n. 25.

23. The problems involved in a discussion of the statue-columns that originally decorated all three portals are so complicated that brief mention of them would be meaningless. I hold to the opinion that they were finished and in place for the dedication of 9 June 1140. As an integral and perhaps the most original part of the portal sculpture, they will ultimately receive the attention they deserve. See Gerson, *West Facade,* 140–61; and Crosby (1987), 192–201.

24. The carved columns that Debret substituted for the statue columns were severely criticized in "Rapport sur la restauration de l'église royale de St Denis," June 1841, fol. 5v, in Dossier de l'Administration 1841–1876, Paris, Archives de la Commission des Monuments historiques. In defending his choice of patterns as appropriate to a twelfth-century facade, Debret wrote that he had visited Chartres in 1837 and made

drawings of the ornament on the west portals. He said he had used some of the patterns decorating the Chartrain colonnettes for the designs on the new columns in the embrasures of the portals, in the belief that the hand responsible for the Chartrain designs had also worked at Saint-Denis: Debret, "Réponse," fol. 19.

25. Stoddard, *West Portals,* 4, 57, pls. III–IV.

26. Ibid., 6, pl. VI, fig. 2. As noted above, the two colonnettes that Stoddard cited as the only remnants of the hypothetical decoration on the intercolonnettes of the embrasures were fragments of those pictured by Le Gentil de la Galaisière on the left jambs of the north and south portals (see above, n. 17).

27. Possibly the surviving vestiges belonged to a frieze of monsters and grotesques such as those intertwining across the embrasures behind the consoles that support the statue-columns of the Porte des Valois in the north transept.

28. For enlarged illustrations, see Crosby (1987), 402–403, figs. K.28–29.

29. On the development of the continuous capital, see John B. Cameron, "The Early Gothic Continuous Capital and Its Precursors," *Gesta* 15 (1976): 143–50.

30. For other illustrations of the abacus friezes, see Crosby (1987), K.25 a–e.

CHAPTER 7

1. The allegory of the Tree of Jesse received special attention at Saint-Denis; it also provided the subject for an entire window in Suger's new choir. The location of the window in the axial chapel of the chevet underscores the importance of the theme. See Arthur Watson, *The Early Iconography of the Tree of Jesse* (London, 1934), 81–88, 112–20; Louis Grodecki, *Les Vitraux de Saint-Denis, étude sur le vitrail au XII siècle* (Corpus Vitrearum Medii Aevi), 1, *France* (Paris, 1976), 71–80; and Crosby et al., *Royal Abbey,* 72, cat. no. 10.

2. Aubert and Beaulieu, *Description raisonée . . . ,* vol. I, *Moyen Age,* 57, cat. nos. 52, 53, 55. The three heads in question range in measurement from 0.20 m. to 0.25 m. The differences, attributable partly to the heights of the surviving headdresses, also result from the recutting of the tops of the original heads and their headdresses. They measure 0.13 m. to 0.155 m. across at eye level and, from the outer corner of one eye to the other, 0.10 m. The comparable measurements of the nineteenth-century heads are 0.155 m. to 0.16 m. at eye level, and 0.10 m. from outer corner to outer corner of the eyes. A comparison shows that the facial style of the twelfth-century heads of the patriarchs closely resembles that of the smaller joined heads of the two Apostles (Fig. 14).

3. [Guilhermy], "Saint-Denis. Restauration," 404, scorned the headdresses as extremely vulgar and iconographically incorrect. He assumed that the restorer had mistaken the figures for musicians of low birth.

   In monumental sculpture, examples of elders with crowns occur at Moissac, on the archivolts of the central door of the royal portal at Chartres, and on the archivolts of the cathedral at Angers.

4. In order to make the most efficient use of space allotted for diagrams, diagrams of

patriarchs J and V had to be sacrificed (compare the schema and Plate I with Plates VIb–IXb). In patriarch J, one inset replaced the head and hair above the voussoir joint; another, almost rectangular in shape, formed the legs from mid-thigh to ankle. The still-mutilated right hand and the instrument he carries show no recutting, nor do his feet or the tip of his beard, left hip, or the outer surface of the left upper thigh. Recutting, moderate but not actually deforming, prevailed everywhere else, but the inset restoring the legs so distorts their forms that the restoration can only be characterized as a disaster.

      Patriarch V also has two insets: one replacing his head, the other patching his left knee. The ends of his beard, the collar, vase, instrument, and both hands and feet escaped recutting, which, however, has affected all of his drapery. Along his shoulders, recutting proved severe enough to reduce their silhouettes and also to diminish both the height and forward projection of the right knee. Elsewhere the recutting blurred the contours of the ridges of the folds but did not affect their arrangements. With these modifications in mind, comparisons citing this figure will have validity if confined to the disposition of the drapery and figure proportions.

5.   Von Borries, "Die Westportale," 145, 153, suggested that the two busts, as well as the disk with the apocalyptic Lamb in the archivolt below, were nineteenth-century inventions.

6.   Assuredly, in a workshop of the size required to implement Suger's projects, assistants must have played a role. Here and elsewhere in the portal, we may reasonably assume that one or more assistants worked with each master and presumably were trained by him, or at least shared his geographical and artistic background. Their presence would account for variations in quality or artistic interest within a master's style—variations detectable, for instance, in figures such as the censing angels nos. XVI and XVII, and in patriarchs E, F, and S.

7.   Bede, *Opera exegetica* pt. 2, 18, *De templo Salomonis, P.L.* 91, cols. 779–80. See also M.-L. Thérèl, "Comment la patrologie peut éclairer l'archéologie; à propos d'Arbre de Jessé et de statues-colonnes de Saint-Denis," *Cahiers de civilisation médiévale* 6 (1963): 145–58.

8.   Schiller, *Iconography,* 1: 23.

9.   Of the twenty-four elders, only patriarchs A and D actually play their instruments. Presumably all the patriarchs wore crowns, as discussed above. By the twelfth century, any single, seated, harp-playing figure with or without a crown, unless otherwise identified within a specific iconographical program, customarily represented King David. Since the archivolt figures conflate the image of patriarchs and elders, the biblical references in the Book of the Apocalypse are as pertinent here as the Old Testament symbolism associated with bare feet and with King David's musicianship—details identifying patriarch A as David. Therefore the following New Testament references, such as those to the harps of the elders, suggest additional layers of meaning for the figures of the patriarch/elders making music: "And I heard a voice from heaven . . . [which] was as the voice of harpers harping on

their harps: And they sung as it were a new canticle before the throne" (Apocalypse 14:2–3); "and them that had overcome the beast . . . having the harps of God: And singing the canticle of Moses, the servant of God, and the canticle of the Lamb, saying: Great and wonderful are thy works, O Lord God Almighty. . . . And after these things I looked; and behold, the temple of the tabernacle of the testimony in heaven was opened" (Apocalypse 15:3–5).

10. Suger, *De administratione,* in Panofsky, ed., *Suger,* 78–79, fig. 8. On the *justa* or Eleanor vase, see volume 3 of Blaise de Montesquiou-Fezensac and Danielle Gaborit-Chopin, *Le Trésor de Saint-Denis* (Paris, 1977), 166, no. 75, pls. 47–48; and Crosby et al., *Royal Abbey,* 112, fig. 36. Now preserved in the Galerie d'Appollon in the Louvre, the vase has a bowl of crystal regarded as "probably Egyptian work of the fourth or fifth century." The gold mounting with jewels and filigree decoration is generally regarded as medieval. Suger recorded that Eleanor of Aquitaine received the vase as a gift from Mitadolus, her grandfather. As a bride Eleanor then gave it to her first husband, Louis VII, who in turn bestowed it on Suger.

11. The instruments represent three basic types. Emanuel Winternitz, the late curator of instruments at the Metropolitan Museum of Art, New York, identified them as follows: "All the instruments with a neck—some plucked and some bowed—are vielles; the instruments of a triangular or nearly triangular shape are harps; those resembling rectangular boxes with strings running across the sound board parallel to the wide side walls are psalteries": Winternitz to Crosby, 15 March 1971. See also Emanuel Winternitz, *Musical Instruments and Their Symbolism in Western Art* (New York, ca. 1967), 29, pls. 11b, 14a, 15c, 23.

12. The sculptor's interest in surface-pattern emerges to an even greater degree in this figure. Yet the deeply undercut hem of the pleats falling from the left hip and the even more undercut, flared hemline of the tunic below enhance the sense of volume and spatial reality which the multiplicity of surface designs tends to suppress in the figure of patriarch A.

13. With the instruments numbered 1. Harp; 2. Psaltery; 3. Vielle, and with the diagram following the lettering in the schema facing Plate I, the composition appears thus:

left archivolts				*right archivolts*	
M^2					Z^2
L^3	K^2			W^3	Y^3
J^1	H^1	G^3	T^3	U^2	V^2
F^3	E^1	D^3	Q^2	R^1	S^3
C^3	B^2	A^1	N^1	O^2	P^3

The eight pairs created by identical instruments are: $A^1 N^1$; $B^2 O^2$; $C^3 P^3$; $E^1 R^1$; $F^3 S^3$; $G^3 T^3$; $L^3 Y^3$; $M^2 Z^2$. Except for Q and D, the remaining figures achieve a pairing, not on opposite sides of the archivolt, but with an adjacent figure as follows: $H^1 J^1$; $K^2 M^2$; $U^2 V^2$; $W^3 Y^3$.

14. For example, although patriarchs B and O both have elongated proportions, patri-

archs A and N balance each other in the visual importance of their active drapery patterns. In the tier above, patriarchs E and F mirror patriarchs R and S both in pose and in placement of the attributes. The rhythm becomes syncopated in the fourth archivolt where the poses of the two uppermost seated figures on the right, patriarchs V and Y, occur in inverse order in the figures of patriarchs J and L on the left side.

15. For practices and procedures followed by medieval masons as well as sculptors at work depicted in manuscripts, see Pierre du Colombier, *Les Chantiers des cathédrales* (Paris, 1959).

16. The multifolds in close succession covering Christ's foreshortened right thigh also differ significantly from the typical leg-drapery of the Apostle Master, who preferred to reveal the smooth contours of the thigh by stretching fabric across the upper surface, often including the bent knee. He underscored those forms by manipulating the fabric into a few encircling folds, frequently in combination with hook folds incised into the flesh or with generously spaced Languedocian folds (see, for example, Apostles nos. 21, 24, 29, 33, Plates IIa and IIIa). In addition the Angel Master's hallmark, a teardrop depression terminating a fold, does not occur in Christ's drapery, nor is there evidence of this artist's characteristic preoccupation with the interplay of curving lines that at once reveal the various planes of the figure and emphasize the overlapping forms.

CHAPTER 8

1. On the mirror image as the architectural principle governing the plans of the western bays and choir, see Crosby (1987), 132, 235, 240.

2. The influence of the Alexandrian's schema has been noted in the wall paintings and mosaics of the Last Judgment scenes in the churches of Sant' Angelo in Formis, Torcello, Reichenau, and Oberzell. On the Alexandrian schema, see D. V. Ainalov, *The Hellenistic Origins of Byzantine Art,* trans. E. and S. Sobolevitch, ed. C. Mango (New Brunswick, N.J., 1961), 33–42.

3. Possibly the Master of the Apostles was responsible for some of the lost statue-columns of the west facade. Stoddard, *West Portals,* 120, suggested that the statue-columns on the left portal showed characteristics of the Master of the Apostles. Yet because the statue-columns are now known primarily through the eighteenth-century engravings, comparisons are risky. We know from the drawing of the figure from the cloister, the statue now in the Metropolitan Museum of Art, that the eighteenth-century aesthetic of the artist pervaded his drawings. To compare the statue and drawing, see Ostoia, "A Statue from Saint-Denis," figures on pp. 300–301 (as in Chapter 1 above, n. 38). Dangerous though comparisons are, some of the Apostle Master's ideas emerge quite strongly through the eighteenth-century bias. Because the drawings suggest differences in figure styles among the three portals, Sauerländer, *Gothic Sculpture,* 381, and Stoddard, *Sculptors,* 115, 120, concluded that the groups of statue-columns in each portal had been carved by a different sculptor.

177

Yet the three figures pictured in Montfaucon, *Les Monumens de la monarchie françoise,* 1, pl. XVI, for the left embrasures of the left portal appear far from homogeneous in style with those for the right embrasures of the same portal.

4. Suger, *De administratione,* in Panofsky, ed., *Suger,* 56–59.

5. Sauerländer, *Gothic Sculpture,* 381. Like other historians of art before him, Sauerländer approached the problem of regional influences from the perspective of the statue-columns, for which he had to rely on the eighteenth-century drawings published by Montfaucon (Fig. 1). In them he saw the Languedoc as the primary source for the statue-columns on the left and central portals, as well as for the jamb-figures on the latter (Plates Xa, XIa). For comparisons, he cited the statues associated with the chapter house of Saint-Etienne, Toulouse. Wilhelm Vöge, also focusing on sources for the concept of statue-columns and their styles, had been the first to suggest influences at Saint-Denis from the art of Languedoc: *Die Anfänge des monumentalen Stiles im Mittelalter* (Strasburg, 1894), 80–90. Emile Mâle, *Religious Art in France—The Twelfth Century; A Study of the Origins of Medieval Iconography,* ed. Harry Bober, trans. M. Mathews (Princeton, N.J., 1987), 178–83, then posited that Suger had summoned "those teams of artists who had wandered all over Languedoc and Aquitaine, who went from Toulouse to Moissac, from Moissac to Beaulieu, and from Beaulieu to Souillac." Mâle's primary interest lay in the migration of iconographical ideas from the Midi to Saint-Denis. Arthur Kingsley Porter, *Romanesque Sculpture of the Pilgrimage Roads* (Boston, 1922), 1, 222–25, in seeking the earlier images that might have inspired the statue-columns on early Gothic portals, extended the search for precursors to Italy (e.g., Ferrara, Cremona, Verona) and Santiago de Compostella. Because his dating of many monuments is no longer accepted, the priorities he assigned to sculptural ensembles and the subsequent migration of artistic concepts from one place to another no longer hold. Nevertheless, his intimate knowledge of the sculpture along the pilgrimage routes and his identification of the work of the Italian sculptor Niccolò as important in the migration of artistic ideas to the Ile-de-France and Saint-Denis deserve the attention and credit that they have not received to date.

6. A detailed analysis of the backgrounds of the artists and other regional influences beyond those cited in the earlier literature that converged in Suger's sculptural atelier are not in the scope of this study. A monograph is in preparation by this author that will treat those aspects of all three western portals and provide the requisite illustrative material supporting the conclusions. See above, Chapter 6, n. 2.

7. Didron, "Achèvement des restaurations," 111, 112–13: "There is not a profile, not a sculpture, no facing of stone in the entire surface of the monument that has not been scraped, modified, compromised. At Saint-Denis, no one . . . is capable of differentiating . . . the ancient from the modern to conserve one and replace the other."

SELECTED BIBLIOGRAPHY

ARCHIVAL SOURCES

Paris, Archives Nationales

"L'Eglise abbatial de Saint-Denis." F^{13} 1293; F^{13} 1295; F^{13} 1296.

Paris, Archives de la Commission des Monuments historiques

Album Debret.

Debret, François. "Réponse aux observations critiques du Rapport de la Commission des
Monuments historiques, adressée à Monsieur le Ministre des Travaux publics au
sujet des travaux de restauration exécutés à l'église royale de St Denis." Seine,
Saint-Denis. Dossier de l'Administration 1841–1876, fols. 15–40. Paris, Archives
de la Commission des Monuments historiques.

Seine, Saint-Denis. Dossier de l'Administration 1841–1876.

———. Registre des attachements de l'église royale de Saint-Denis. "Statuaire et sculpture, 1835–1842.

Paris, Bibliothèque Nationale

Gautier, Ferdinand-Albert. "Journal qui fait suite à Félibien." Ms. fr. 11681.

Guilhermy, Ferdinand François, baron de. "Notes." Nouv. acq. ms. fr. 1161–1162.

Von Borries, Johann Eckart. "Die Westportale der Abteikirche von Saint-Denis. Versuch
einer Rekonstruktion." Ph.D. diss., Universität Hamburg, 1947.

PRINTED PRIMARY SOURCES

Augustine. *Contra Cresconium grammaticum partis Donati.* In *Patrologia latina cursus
completus,* ed. J. P. Migne, vol. 43. Paris, 1841, cols. 445–594.

———. *De Trinitate* 1, 31. In *Patrologia latina cursus completus,* ed. J.-P. Migne, vol. 42.
Paris, 1841, cols. 819–1098.

Bede. *Opera exigetica,* pt. 2, *De templo Salomonis.* In *Patrologia latina cursus completus,*
ed. J.-P. Migne, vol. 91. Paris, 1850, cols. 735–808.

[Fortunatus]. *Passio sanctorum martyrum Dionysii, Rustici et Eleutherii* [known also as the *Gloriosae*]. In *Monumenta germaniae historica,* ed. Bruno Krusch. Auct. antiq., 4, pt. 2. Berlin, 1885, 101–105.

Hilduinus abbas s. Dionysii. *Areopagitica sive Sancti Dionysii vita.* In *Patrologia latina cursus completus,* ed. J.-P. Migne, vol. 106. Paris, 1851, cols. 13–24.

Lecoy de la Marche, Auguste, ed. *Oeuvres complètes de Suger recueillies, annotées et publiées d'après les manuscrits pour la Société de l'Histoire de France.* Paris, 1867.

Ryan, Granger, and Helmut Ripperger, eds. *The Golden Legend of Jacobus de Voragine.* New York, 1969.

Suger. *Liber de rebus in administratione sua gestis.* In Panofsky, ed., *Suger,* 40–81.

———. *Libellus alter de consecratione ecclesiae Sancti Dionysii.* In Panofsky, ed., *Suger,* 82–121.

———. *Ordinatio A.D. MCXL vel MCXLI confirmata.* In Panofsky, ed., *Suger,* 122–37.

Willelmus. *Litterae encyclicae conventus Sancti Dionysii de morte Sugerii abbatis.* In *Oeuvres complètes de Suger,* ed. A. Lecoy de la Marche. Paris, 1867, pp. 405–406.

BOOKS AND ARTICLES

Ainalov, D. V. *The Hellenistic Origins of Byzantine Art.* Trans. E. and S. Sobolevitch, ed. Cyril Mango. New Brunswick, N.J., 1961.

Aubert, Marcel, and Michèle Beaulieu. *Musée National du Louvre. Description raisonnée des sculptures du Moyen Age, de la Renaissance, et des temps modernes.* Vol. I, *Moyen Age.* Paris, 1950.

Blum, Pamela Z. "The Lateral Portals of the West Facade of the Abbey Church of Saint-Denis: Archaeological and Iconographical Considerations." In Gerson, ed., *Abbot Suger,* pp. 199–228.

Cartellieri, Otto. *Abt Suger von Saint-Denis, 1081–1151.* Berlin, 1898.

Conway, W. Martin. "The Abbey of Saint-Denis and Its Ancient Treasures." *Archaeologia* 66, 2nd ser. (1915): 103–58.

Crosby, Sumner McKnight. *L'Abbaye royale de Saint-Denis.* Paris, 1953.

———. *The Abbey of St. Denis 475–1122.* Vol. I. New Haven, Conn., 1942.

———. *The Apostle Bas-Relief at Saint-Denis.* New Haven, Conn., 1972.

———. "An International Workshop in the Twelfth Century." *Cahiers d'histoire mondiale* 10 (1966): 19–30.

———. *The Royal Abbey of Saint-Denis from Its Beginnings to the Death of Suger, 475–1151.* Edited and completed by Pamela Z. Blum. New Haven, Conn., 1987.

———. "The West Portals of Saint-Denis and the Saint-Denis Style." *Gesta* 9/2 (1970): 1–11.

Crosby, Sumner McKnight, and Pamela Z. Blum. "Le Portail central de la façade occidentale de Saint-Denis." Trans. D. Thibaudat. *Bulletin monumental* 131/3 (1973): 209–66.

Crosby, Sumner McKnight, Jane Hayward, Charles Little, and William Wixom, eds. *The Royal Abbey of Saint-Denis in the Time of Abbot Suger (1122–1151).* New York, 1981.

Delcourt, A. *J. S. Brun. Sculpteur statuaire. Ancien pensionnaire de Rome. Saint-Denis. L'Arc de Triomphe de l'Etoile. Le Palais de Justice de Rouen.* Paris, 1846.

Didron, A. N. "Achèvement des restaurations de Saint-Denis." *Annales archéologiques* 5 (1846): 107–13.

Doublet, Dom F. Jacques. *Histoire de l'abbaye de S. Denys en France.* Paris, 1625.

Félibien, Michel. *Histoire de l'abbaye royale de Saint-Denis en France.* Paris, 1706.

Le Gentil de la Galaisière, Guillaume J. H. J. B. "Observations sur plusieurs monumens gothiques que j'ai remarqués dans cette capitale, sur lesquels sont gravés les signes du zodiaque et quelques hiéroglyphes egyptiens relatifs à la religion d'Isis." *Histoire de l'Académie Royale des Sciences, année 1788 avec les mémoires de mathématique & de physique pour la même année 1788* 90 (Paris, 1791): 390–438.

Gerson, Paula Lieber. "The Lintels of the West Facade of Saint-Denis." *Journal of the Society of Architectural Historians* 34/3 (1975): 187–97.

———. "Suger as Iconographer: The Central Portal of the West Facade of Saint-Denis." In Gerson, ed., *Abbot Suger,* pp. 183–98.

———. *The West Facade of Saint-Denis. An Iconographic Study.* Ph.D. diss., Columbia University, New York, 1970. Ann Arbor, Mich. (UMI, 1970, no. 73-26, 428).

———, ed. *Abbot Suger and Saint-Denis. A Symposium.* New York, 1986.

Goldscheider, Cécile. "Les Origines des portails à statues-colonnes." *Bulletin des musées de France* 6/7 (1946): 22–25.

Goldschmidt, Adolph. *Die Elfenbeinskulpturen aus der Zeit der karolingischen und sächsischen Kaiser.* 4 vols. Paris, 1914–1926.

Guilhermy, Ferdinand François, baron de. "Restauration de l'église royale de Saint-Denis." *Annales archéologiques* 5 (1846): 200–215.

[Guilhermy, Ferdinand François, baron de.] "Saint-Denis. Restauration de l'église royale." *Annales archéologiques* 1 (1844): 400–411.

Kidson, Peter. "Panofsky, Suger, and St Denis." *Journal of the Warburg and Courtauld Institutes* 50 (1987): 1–17.

Little, Charles T. "Monumental Sculpture at Saint-Denis under the Patronage of Abbot Suger." In *The Royal Abbey of Saint-Denis in the Time of Suger (1122–1151),* ed. Sumner McKnight Crosby et al. New York, 1981, pp. 25–29.

Mâle, Emile. "La Part de Suger dans la création de l'iconographie du Moyen Age." *Revue de l'art ancien et moderne* 35 (1914): 92–102, 161–68, 253–62, 339–49.

Montesquiou-Fezensac, Blaise, comte de, with Danielle Gaborit-Chopin. *Le Trésor de Saint-Denis.* 3 vols. Paris, 1973–1977.

Montfaucon, Bernard de. *Les Monumens de la monarchie françoise qui comprennent l'histoire de France . . .* 5 vols. Paris, 1729–1733.

Morrison, Kathryn A. "The Eighteenth-Century `Restoration' of the West Portals of Saint-Denis and the Problem of the Lintels." *Journal of the British Archaeological Association* 139 (1986): 134–42.

Panofsky, Erwin, ed. and trans. *Abbot Suger. On the Abbey Church of St.-Denis and Its Art Treasures.* Princeton, N.J., 1946. 2nd edition: Gerda Panofsky-Soergel, ed. Princeton, N.J., 1979.

181

Prache, Anne. *Ile-de-France romane.* La Nuit des temps 60. Zodiaque, 1983.

Pressouyre, Léon. "Une Tête de reine du portail central de Saint-Denis." *Gesta* 15 (1976): 151–60.

Quarré, Pierre. "L'Abbé Lebeuf et l'interprétation du portail de Saint-Bénigne de Dijon." In *Actes de Congrès Lebeuf* (Auxerre, 1960): 1–7.

Réau, Louis. *Les Monuments détruits de l'art français.* 2 vols. Paris, 1959.

Ross, Marvin Chauncey. "Monumental Sculptures from Saint-Denis. An Identification of Fragments from the Portal." *Journal of the Walters Art Gallery* 3 (1940): 90–109.

Rudolph, Conrad. *Artistic Change at Saint-Denis: Abbot Suger's Program and the Early Twelfth-Century Controversy over Art.* Princeton, N.J., 1990.

Sauerländer, Willibald. *Gothic Sculpture in France 1140–1270.* Trans. Janet Sondheimer. New York, 1972.

———. "Sculpture on Early Gothic Churches: The State of Research and Open Questions." *Gesta* 9/2 (1970): 34.

Saxl, Fritz. "Frühes Christentum und spätes Heidentum in ihren künsterlischen Ausdruckformen." *Wiener Jahrbuch für Kunstgeschichte* n.f. 2 (16) (1923): 63–121.

———. *English Sculptures of the Twelfth Century.* Ed. Hanns Swarzenski. Boston, 1952.

Scheller, R. W. *A Survey of Medieval Model Books.* Haarlem, 1963.

Schiller, Gertrud. *Iconography of Christian Art.* 2 vols. Trans. J. Seligman. London, 1972.

Stoddard, Whitney. *The West Portals of Saint-Denis and Chartres: Sculpture in the Ile-de-France from 1140 to 1190.* Cambridge, Mass., 1952.

———. *The Sculptors of the West Portals of Chartres Cathedral.* New York, London, 1987.

Thérèl, Marie-Louise. "Comment la patrologie peut éclairer l'archéologie. A propos d'Arbre de Jessé et de statues-colonnes de Saint-Denis." *Cahiers de civilisation médiévale* 6 (1963): 145–58.

Vieillard-Troïekouroff, May. "Les Zodiaques parisiens sculptés d'après Le Gentil de la Galaisière, astronome du XVIIIe siècle." *Mémoires de la Société nationale des Antiquaires de France* 4, 9e ser. (1968). (Paris, 1969): 161–94.

Vitry, Paul, and Gaston Brière. *L'Eglise abbatiale royale de Saint-Denis et ses tombeaux. Notice historique et archéologique.* Paris, 1925.

Watson, Arthur. *The Early Iconography of the Tree of Jesse.* London, 1934.

Winternitz, Emanuel. *Musical Instruments and Their Symbolism in Western Art.* New York, ca. 1967. 2nd edition, New Haven, Conn., 1979.

Zinn, Grover A. "Suger, Theology, and the Pseudo-Dionysian Tradition." In Gerson, ed., *Abbot Suger,* pp. 31–40.

Designer: Scott Hudson, Marquand Books, Inc.
Text: Versailles Light
Display: Trajan
Compositor: G & S Typesetters, Inc.
Printer: Thomson-Shore, Inc.
Binder: Thomson-Shore, Inc.